INTO THE UNKNOWN

INTO THE UNKNOWN
Leadership Lessons from Lewis & Clark's
Daring Westward Adventure

JACK ULDRICH

AMACOM AMERICAN MANAGEMENT ASSOCIATION
NEW YORK ✦ ATLANTA ✦ BRUSSELS ✦ CHICAGO ✦ MEXICO CITY
SAN FRANCISCO ✦ SHANGHAI ✦ TOKYO ✦ TORONTO ✦ WASHINGTON, D.C.

This publication is designed to provide accurate and authoritative information in regard to the subject matter covered. It is sold with the understanding that the publisher is not engaged in rendering legal, accounting, or other professional service. If legal advice or other expert assistance is required, the services of a competent professional person should be sought.

Library of Congress Cataloging-in-Publication Data

Uldrich, Jack, 1964-
   Into the unknown : leadership lessons from Lewis & Clark's daring westward adventure / Jack Uldrich.
      p. cm.
Includes bibliographical references and index.
   ISBN 0-8144-0816-8
   1. Leadership—Case studies. 2. Organizational commitment—Case studies. 3. Employee motivation—Case studies. 4. Teams in the workplace—Case studies. 5. Lewis and Clark Expedition (1804–1806) I. Title: Leadership lessons from Lewis & Clark's daring westward adventure. II. Lewis, Meriwether, 1774–1809. III. Clark, William, 1770–1838. IV. Title.

HD57.7.U43 2004
658.4'092—dc22

                                                    2003025551

Printing number
10 9 8 7 6 5 4 3 2 1

CONTENTS

❖ ❖ ❖

PREFACE

Since I am a business consultant in the emerging field of nanotechnology—and the author of a book on the topic—the decision to write my next book on the subject of Lewis and Clark may appear odd. It is not.

In my job, I am often called upon to speak before businesses, trade associations, government agencies, and nonprofit organizations about nanotechnology and its implications for the future. I tell audiences that nanotechnology is fueling exponential advances in computing power, data storage, disease prevention, cancer treatment, material science, molecular manufacturing, and energy production. The conclusion of all of my presentations can be summed up in this one simple sentence: The future is going to be radically different, and to prosper, people need to embrace change and become comfortable dealing with the unknown.

Early in my speaking career, I could tell that by the end of my talk, some people in the audience were so overwhelmed by the massive amount of change I was forecasting that they just sort of shut down mentally and tuned out my message. Most, however, were more concerned about how they could adapt to a future that, in many ways, is so unknowable.

As I struggled to find a better way to communicate how exciting the future was going to be and how people could prosper in these changing times, a friend suggested that I read Stephen Ambrose's book on Lewis and Clark, *Undaunted Courage*. Needing a reprieve from my technical readings on nanotechnology, I readily heeded his advice. Since then, I have been hooked on Lewis and Clark. In the process of learning as much as possible about them and their journey, I discovered that the captains, in exploring the interior of the North American continent and reaching the Pacific, had conquered the unknown. They did so without knowing how long their trip would take or what skills or equipment would prove helpful; and they had only the vaguest idea of the obstacles, challenges, or difficulties that awaited them. In spite of all this, they not only were successful, they found their journey enjoyable and rewarding.

For me, Lewis and Clark became the perfect metaphor for individuals grappling with change and a fear of the unknown. But as I researched their lives and continued to comb their extensive journals documenting in vivid detail their amazing journey, I soon realized that Lewis and Clark were much more than just a useful metaphor. The two captains illuminated a path—a path based on ten principles—that people, even today, can use to approach the unknown.

It is my hope that readers will use this book as a practical guide for thinking about, and preparing themselves and their organizations for, the future. For although Lewis and Clark's story is now 200 years old, the principles upon which their success was based are timeless, and I am confident that their story will continue to resonate with future generations.

I hope you enjoy the book, and I invite readers to contact me with your stories of how Lewis and Clark's journey and their leadership principles helped you and your organization deal with the uncertainty of the future.

Note About Sources and Spellings

Quotes attributed to Meriwether Lewis and William Clark come primarily from *The Journals of the Lewis and Clark Expedition*, edited by Gary Moulton. To the greatest extent possible, the original spellings that Lewis and Clark used in their journals have also been retained. When a source other than the journals is used, it is either referenced in the text or footnoted.

Acknowledgments

I begin by thanking my good friend Rolf Nordstrom for unwittingly setting me on the course to write this book by recommending that I read Stephen Ambrose's *Undaunted Courage*. Special thanks go to my editor, Adrienne Hickey, at AMACOM; Douglas Puchowski, the development editor; and my literary agent, Greg Dinkin, for redirecting me when necessary and constantly pushing me to make the story of Lewis and Clark more relevant to today's—and tomorrow's—audiences. The book is better as a result of their efforts.

The book, of course, would not have been possible without the dedication and tireless effort of all the professional and amateur scholars who have devoted so much time to researching and documenting the lives of Lewis and Clark and the Corps of Discovery. I am indebted to their work. I only hope I have provided some new insight or perspective on Lewis and Clark's incredible journey. It goes without saying that any mistakes or errors in this book are my responsibility alone.

Finally, I wish to thank my wife, Cindy, and our two children, Meghan and Sean. Their unconditional love and support sustained me through the many long hours it took to finish this book. I could not have done it without them.

Jack Uldrich
jack@nanoveritas.com
Minneapolis, Minnesota
March 2004

PART ONE

✤ ✤ ✤

Why Lewis and Clark Matter

LEWIS AND CLARK
Leaders for Their Time—and Ours

*Never look down to test the ground before
taking your next step; only he who keeps his
eye fixed on the far horizon will find his
right road.*
—Dag Hammarskjöld, Secretary General
of the United Nations (1953–1961)

On August 12, 1805, Meriwether Lewis climbed the eastern slope of the Continental Divide toward the realization of a lifelong goal. He was on the verge of becoming the first American to view with his own eyes the fabled Northwest Passage—an all-water route that connected the Pacific and Atlantic oceans. It was a dream as old as Christopher Columbus, and the discovery of the passage was President Thomas Jefferson's primary motivation for authorizing the journey of the Corps of Discovery. But when Lewis reached the summit and gazed west, what he beheld was not a river running westward toward the Pacific but rather more mountains—mountains as far as the eye could see. It was at that precise moment that he knew the future was going to be totally different from anything he or Captain William Clark had expected. Still, Lewis and Clark and the Corps of Discovery proceeded on. Their willingness to "proceed on"—a phrase that is repeated numerous times in the captains' journals—in the face of adversity and uncertainty lies at the heart of this book.

Two centuries later, Lewis and Clark's story still captures the public's imagination. It has been called "our national epic" and "America's own odyssey," and an estimated 30 million people are expected to retrace some portion of the journey over the course of the bicentennial celebration (May 14, 2004, to September 23, 2006).

Why?

Part of the reason is that the journey exemplifies the best of the American tradition: a diverse group of people exploring new areas and coming together as a team, in the face of tremendous odds, to conquer those uncharted areas. Another reason is that it is simply an incredible story packed with more action, intrigue, and suspense than the best Hollywood blockbuster. But beyond the inspirational and action-packed story itself, people are drawn to the expedition because it holds timeless lessons they can still learn from today. Foremost among these lessons is what the expedition's two co-commanders, Meriwether Lewis and William Clark, can teach us about leadership and dealing with the unknown—especially when it turns out to be far different from anything we had come to expect.

The leadership of Lewis and Clark, like the binding of a good book, provided the expedition its structure and moved the members of the Corps of Discovery 8,000 miles over the course of 863 days toward the actualization of a goal that was, in its time, the equivalent of man landing on the moon.

This book, unlike most books about Lewis and Clark and their expedition, will not attempt to recount their journey in chronological fashion. Lewis and Clark's own journals, which have been edited at different times by Nicholas Biddle, Reuben Gold Thwaites, Bernard DeVoto, and, most recently, Gary Moulton, are by far the best source for experiencing and learning about the journey. Other books such as Stephen Ambrose's *Undaunted Courage*, David Lavender's *The Way to the Western Sea*, and James Ronda's *Lewis and Clark Among the Indians* are also informative and compelling narratives of the expedition. Rather, this book will examine the expedition through the lens of leadership and apply the extraordinary lessons of Lewis and Clark's leadership to today's rapidly changing and often unknowable business environment. (For those readers not familiar with the key events of Lewis and Clark's expedition, an abridged account of their journey is provided in the next section.)

In spite of a 200-year gap, the challenges Lewis and Clark faced and those confronting today's leaders are more similar than one might initially expect. The twenty-first century is a time of accelerating, almost exponential change. Advances in computer electronics, telecommunications, and medicine are announced every day. Genomics, nanotechnology, wireless technologies, the Internet, fuel cells, solar cells, DNA analysis, the sequencing of the human genome, stem cell research, voice recognition technology, and even the advancement of knowledge itself are propelling us faster and faster downriver, and, like Lewis and Clark, we don't know what's around the next bend. Similarly, the relentless force of globalization is introducing us to new cultures and hurling unexpected challenges and opportunities at us to the same degree that Lewis and Clark had to respond to—and deal with— dozens of new and different Indian tribes and cultures.

How can we prepare for this future? What skills will we need? What tools? What equipment? Where do we even start? These are the very questions Lewis and Clark asked themselves, and we can look to them for inspiration. Who better to turn to than those who have already climbed seemingly impassable mountains, rafted untamable rivers, and explored forests full of unknown, wild, and dangerous threats? Who better to look to for guidance when dealing with the unknown than those who have already demonstrated that they were capable of successfully conquering the unknown?

There are myriad parallels that make Lewis and Clark useful and poignant examples for today's business executives. Like today's business leaders, Lewis and Clark were driven by an important mission and were determined to succeed at all costs. They also knew how to:

→ Think strategically

→ Surround themselves with good people

→ Make tough and timely decisions

→ Manage resources

→ Motivate their team

→ Interact with different cultures

→ Assimilate vast amounts of information from a variety of sources

→ Balance long-term interests with short-term realities

→ Learn from their mistakes

→ Try new approaches

→ Handle adversity

This book will help anyone struggling with these same issues and will provide concrete examples from the experiences of Lewis and Clark on how they handled and overcame similar challenges.

A Refresher

Before exploring the leadership lessons, it will be useful to provide some refresher material on the two leaders. Both men stood six feet tall, possessed extraordinary physical stamina, and were experienced frontiersmen. Lewis, the second son of a Virginia landowner, was twenty-nine years old at the beginning of the expedition. He possessed more formal education than Clark, and served six years with the U.S. Army on the western frontier. In 1801, he was appointed by President Jefferson to serve as his personal secretary. Lewis held the position until he assumed co-command of the expedition. By all accounts, he was cool, reserved, and generally humorless, and suffered from bouts of depression. He was also a skilled hunter and superb botanist. He was highly motivated, disciplined, dedicated, fair, intelligent, and visionary.

William Clark was four years older than Lewis and the sixth son of a Virginia plantation owner and the younger brother of George Clark, a Revolutionary War hero. He joined the Army in 1789 and three years later became an officer and fought in several campaigns. In 1795, he briefly served as Lewis's commanding officer in an infantry rifle unit. He was a superior boatman and cartographer and possessed immense practical intelligence. In contrast to Lewis, Clark was warm and engaging, had an easy manner, and was more popular with the men.

Their skills and personalities were perfectly compatible, and their trust and confidence in each other complete and unequivocal. Together, the two arguably made the most successful leadership team in American history. They are, as Stephen Ambrose wrote in *Undaunted Courage*, largely known as "Lewisandclark."

CURIOUS AND INTIMATE

Through their journals, we come to learn not just of Lewis and Clark's heroic feats, we come to know them as people. Part of the their charm and interest, we learn, is their childlike curiosity. For example, we are there on the prairie as Lewis and Clark and other members of the party spend the better part of the day poking sticks and pouring barrels of water down holes in an effort to capture a prairie dog, which they then sent back to President Jefferson. We are there as they fill the beak of a pelican with water and record that it can hold five gallons. We note with slightly less interest that a jackrabbit leaped twenty-one feet, that a rattlesnake had a total of 221 scuta on its belly and fifty-three on its tail, and that it took thirty-six hours for two spoonfuls of water to evaporate on the plains of South Dakota.

At other times, they share with us the mundane details of daily life that help us come to know them almost as friends. We feel their discomfort when a new diet of roots and salmon causes them to become "[s]o full of wind" that they are scarcely "able to breathe all night." We can sense Clark's annoyance at being kept awake at night by the sound of beavers smacking their tails against the water and, at another time, of being unable to sleep because of rutting bison. We read with some awkwardness as Lewis, writing about the revealing dress of female Clatsop Indians, notes that their "battery of Venus is not altogether impervious to the inquisitive and penetrating eye," and we marvel at Clark's wonderful flexibility with the English language—according to Robert Betts, the author of *In Search of York*, Clark spells the word *Sioux* twenty-seven different ways.[1] (Ironically, today's common spelling was not among them.) We share their surprise at encountering Native Americans near the Pacific who know enough of the English language to say "damned rascal" and "son of a bitch." We laugh with Clark when, after eating the blubber of a giant beached whale, he thanks Providence for sending "this monster to be swallowed by us instead of swallowing us as Jonah's did." We share their fun as they have foot races against the Nez Percé Indians, play the game "prison" (a precursor to today's national pastime, baseball), and drink whiskey and dance to a fiddle around a campfire.

THE CORPS OF DISCOVERY

Lewis and Clark's greatness would not have occurred but for the men, and one woman, who accompanied them on their journey. It is worthwhile to highlight some of the more noteworthy members. Sacagawea, the young Shoshone Indian teenager who carried her infant son, Jean Baptiste or "Pomp," on her back for 5,000 miles, is perhaps the best known. Her husband, Toussaint Charbonneau, the oldest man on the expedition, was hired as an interpreter and later became known, rather unfairly, for his cowardly behavior. York, Clark's black slave, was by all accounts a full member of the team and fulfilled his share of the daily responsibilities with quiet competence.

The team also consisted of George Droulliard, the highly skilled civilian hunter and interpreter; Sergeant John Ordway, the unit's top soldier; George Shannon, the group's youngest member; Private Joseph Whitehouse, the tailor; Sergeant Patrick Gass, the carpenter; John Shields, the blacksmith; Silas Goodrich, the fisherman; the very capable Field brothers; Pierre Cruzatte, the one-eyed, fiddle-playing boatman; and John Colter, the competent reconnaissance man.

BATTLING THE ELEMENTS

To put the entire book in perspective, it is useful to briefly review some of the challenges they overcame and the hardships they endured. Immediately upon setting out on their journey from Camp Dubois—located near present-day Wood River, Illinois, and sometimes referred to by other writers and historians as Camp Wood—on May 14, 1804, the Corps of Discovery rowed, sailed, pushed, and pulled themselves up the mighty Missouri River, whose swift and powerful current, like a giant fire hose, was unrelenting in its attempt to push them back into the Mississippi River. Collapsing riverbanks, shifting sandbars, and massive uprooted trees were a regular danger and threatened constant catastrophe. So exhausting was the effort that the members of the expedition, on average, devoured nine pounds of meat a day and consumed 6,000 calories.[2]

On the plains near today's Nebraska, sandstorms were so intense that the men felt as if they were "compelled to eat, drink, and breathe" the sand. In what is the present-day South Dakota, the Corps of Discovery, under the cover of moonlight, moved camp only minutes before the land under them crumbled into the river. In North Dakota, raging prairie fires engulfed huge swaths of land and killed two Indians who were near the party. During their winter at Fort Mandan, near what is today Bismarck, North Dakota, the expedition suffered through subzero temperatures so cold that small cottonwood trees exploded.[3] In the spring, as they traversed land that's now part of Montana, they waded up to their armpits in freezing cold water. In the summer months, they endured heat spells so intense that men dropped from heat stroke and suffered under the hot, intense sun that darkened their skin so much they were forced to roll up their sleeves to convince the Native Americans that they were white men. And if the sun wasn't beating down on them from above, prickly pear cactuses were puncturing their leather moccasins and swelling their feet, making it difficult to walk.

Near the Great Falls of Montana they survived a hailstorm that left many of them bloodied, and the ensuing thunderstorm created a flash flood that threatened William Clark, Sacagawea, and her baby with being swept over an eighty-seven-foot waterfall. They endured an eighteen-mile trek that required them to portage thousands of pounds of food and equipment. Shortly thereafter, they hiked over treacherous mountains and had to pass through snow that was, at times, fifteen feet deep. At this point in the journey, they were pushed to the brink of starvation and were so famished they were reduced to eating candles.

After reaching the Columbia River basin, the expedition survived quicksand and rafted down whitewater rapids so violent the native Indians deemed the trip suicidal. Upon nearing the Pacific, they were drenched with rain for eleven straight days and became so wet their leather clothing began to disintegrate on their bodies. On other days the wind was so strong and the fog so thick they could not move. And when they finally were able to make the final push for the Pacific, they encountered colossal 200-foot pieces of driftwood that threatened to crush them and swells so high they made the men sick.

The Corps of Discovery's battles were not limited to Mother Nature's elements, however. Her creatures—large and small— were also a constant menace. They had dozens of run-ins with rattlesnakes and were besieged with lice. The air was, at times, so thick with mosquitoes and gnats that the party had to cover themselves in bear grease and stand in the heavy smoke of a campfire to escape their relentless torment. Ferocious grizzly bears roamed the territory and sent them scampering over twenty-foot cliffs, hiding in bushes, and climbing up trees to escape their wrath. Stampeding buffalo nearly trampled Lewis and Clark to death one night while they slept, and on another occasion a party member was attacked and bitten by a wolf.

And, as if to add insult to injury, throughout all of these trials dysentery, malaria, boils, and a handful of other illnesses plagued the expedition team. Life's other minor nuisances—twisted ankles, bruises, knife and ax cuts, as well as the occasional poisoning— added to their pain and discomfort.

O! THE JOY

In spite of all the hardships and difficulties, the members of the expedition encountered incredible things. Along the way they saw boundless prairies filled with vast herds of free-roaming buffalo, seemingly endless mountain ranges capped with majestic snow-covered peaks, and the rich, dense rain forests of the Pacific Northwest. They witnessed huge chunks of earth collapsing into the river as though the earth was dissolving "like sugar." There were canyons and cliffs of unbelievable grandeur and trees that soared to unimaginable heights. They were the first Americans of European ancestry to see a prairie dog, a magpie, a pronghorn, a coyote, and salmon in water so clear that the fish could be seen at a depth of twenty feet. Near the Pacific, they watched in awe as a California condor glided high overhead and stood in amazement at the sight of a gigantic beached whale.

They were also the first Americans to stand astride the "heretofore deemed endless" Missouri River, the first to peer over the Continental Divide, traverse the Bitterroot Mountains, and descend the rapids of the Columbia River. And, of course, they were the first white men to see the Great Falls of Montana, the Rocky Mountains, and the Pacific Ocean, which was captured in William Clark's immortal writing, "Ocian in view. O! the joy."

FRIEND OR FOE

To have had the opportunity to witness all of these things was not merely the result of Lewis and Clark's and the Corps of Discovery's singular talents. There is little disagreement among scholars that without food, horses, guidance, and the general goodwill of the Indian nations they encountered along the way, the expedition would not have succeeded.

In the winter of 1804–1805, the Mandan and Hidatsa Indians allowed the party to camp near their village and provided them with valuable military protection and even more valuable food. In the famous words of "Big White," the Mandan chief, also known as Shekeke, "If we eat, you shall eat; if we starve, you must starve." The Mandan and Hidatsa also shared useful information about what the land to the west held in store for the Corps of Discovery. Later in the expedition, the Shoshone Indians traded horses to the Corps of Discovery that were absolutely vital for getting over the Bitterroots. And on the other side of the mountains, the Nez Percé Indians provided them with food and canoes. Only in July 1806, when Lewis and a small party encountered the Blackfeet Indians on the return journey, did they have a deadly encounter with native Indians.

LUCK

Throughout their many encounters, Lewis and Clark and the Corps of Discovery also had a string of unbelievable luck that Clark could only attribute to divine intervention. It started with a close call—months before the journey even officially got under way—when Lewis accidentally fired a rifle that nearly killed a woman, and ended with another near disaster averted, when the one-eyed, fiddle-playing Pierre Cruzatte mistook Lewis for an elk and shot him in the buttocks. In between, one researcher figured the expedition encountered fifty-four additional life-threatening incidents.[4] Yet along the way only one man died, Sergeant Charles Floyd, and his death—believed to be caused by a burst appendix—could not have been prevented by the best doctors of the time.

In the end, however, there is no other way to explain certain events—the coincidence of bumping into Sacagawea's brother, Cameahwait, the Shoshone Indian chieftain upon whom they were going to have to rely for horses to cross the mountains, or the saving words of an old Nez Percé Indian woman, who told her tribe not to kill the party—than to attribute them to extraordinary good luck.

BUT IT ALL COMES BACK TO LEADERSHIP

To say that the expedition's success was solely the result of luck or rested entirely on the goodwill of the Indians would be the equivalent of saying that anyone can prepare a great meal if given the right ingredients. It just isn't so. Great chefs can take the same ingredients provided an ordinary chef and produce extraordinary results; and when presented with limited resources, they can still produce very satisfactory results. So it was with Lewis and Clark.

They were the masterminds behind the expedition's success, and their leadership skills lie at the heart of the mission's extraordinary accomplishments. For in the end, they were more than soldiers, naturalists, cartographers, diplomats, or even explorers. First and foremost, they were leaders. Private Whitehouse's eloquent quote about the captains' skill, courage, and humanity filling "the breasts of the men who were under their command . . . and the President of the United States not misplacing his judgment when he appointed them to command this party" is a fitting tribute to their leadership skills.

A short review of the breadth and scope of Lewis and Clark's considerable skills as leaders is revealing.

→ They were ordered to map, study, and describe the region, as well as establish diplomatic relations with the Indians and depict their cultures, languages, politics, health, farming practices, and religious beliefs. Yet, in spite of these significant daily responsibilities, Lewis and Clark were not above getting out of the boat and pushing it upriver, or "swinging their pack" to shoulder their share of the daily burden.

→ They pushed their men to the brink of physical exhaustion on numerous occasions—such as during the portage around the Great Falls—but had the good sense to exercise patience and wait for nearly a month for the snow to melt before crossing back over the Bitterroots on their return trip.

→ They possessed enough confidence in their judgment to override the opinion of every person in the expedition and make the correct decision at a critical fork in the river, yet had enough respect for their team to allow every person—including Sacagawea and York—to vote on the location of their winter camp.

→ They demonstrated the internal fortitude to listen to their men voice concerns when confronted with the prospect of starvation, but never once considered turning back and only displayed the most invincible optimism.

→ They constantly employed their vast knowledge of botany, history, language, medicine, and science, but were always willing to delegate when appropriate and hire experts as necessary.

→ They could administer a hundred lashes as punishment if necessary, but showed real compassion when Sergeant Floyd was dying and Sacagawea lay deathly ill.

→ They could upbraid their men for lapses of judgment during the day, but at the end of the day would reward them by naming rivers and streams in their honor.

→ They were coldly calculating when they pressed on after a valuable soldier went missing for eleven days, but compassionate enough to offer to raise Sacagawea's young son, Pomp, when the expedition was over—as Clark did.

→ They prepared meticulously and ran out of only three items (trading beads, tobacco, and whiskey), but when times got tough they literally traded the jackets off their back for a canoe and ordered their men to barter their shirt buttons for food.

→ They paid the greatest attention to their daily surroundings, including penning a 1,000-word description of the magpie, but never once lost sight of the "big picture" or the real goal: to find the most navigable all-water route to the Pacific and report back to President Jefferson.

→ They made serious mistakes, such as the failed "iron boat experiment," which cost them twelve days during the height of the best traveling season, but never stopped learning and always stayed open to new ways of doing things.

→ They possessed enough discipline to hold their fire during a tense standoff with the Sioux, but were flexible enough to allow the enlisted soldiers to decide on the punishment their fellow soldiers should receive for various infractions.

In the end, Meriwether Lewis and William Clark were able to adapt and remain flexible in the daily administration of their leadership responsibilities because they had a solid foundation of ten principles from which to operate. Those principles were:

1. Passionate Purpose: The Principle of a Higher Calling

2. Productive Partnering: The Principle of Shared Leadership

3. Future Think: The Principle of Strategic Preparation

4. Honoring Differences: The Principle of Diversity

5. Equitable Justice: The Principle of Compassionate Discipline

6. Absolute Responsibility: The Principle of Leading from the Front

7. Meaningful Mentoring: The Principle of Learning from Others

8. Realistic Optimism: The Principle of Positive Thinking

9. Rational Risk: The Principle of Aggressive Analysis

10. Cultivating a Corps of Discovery: The Principle of Developing Team Spirit

PROCEED ON

At the beginning of their journey, Lewis and Clark had so little knowledge of what to expect that they believed the Rocky Mountains would be similar in size to the modest and gentle slopes of the Blue Ridge Mountains. They assumed it would take only a half-day portage from the Missouri headwaters to the Columbia River (not 220 miles primarily over rugged mountains). They thought they might actually encounter prehistoric mastodons roaming the plains and find volcanoes, mountains of pure salt, and even the mythical lost tribe of Welsh Indians.

Yet to their immense credit, when the future turned out to be fundamentally different from what they expected, they simply "proceeded on." They proceeded on knowing that there were no reinforcements. They proceeded on knowing that they could not order more supplies. They proceeded on even when it was apparent they were not going to achieve the goal of finding a "practical" all-water route to the Pacific.

What Lewis and Clark Mean to America

We are much richer because they did proceed on. The first verse of "America the Beautiful" captures one element of what Lewis and Clark mean to America:

> O beautiful for spacious skies
> For amber waves of grain,
> For purple mountain majesties
> Above the fruited plain!
>
> America! America!
> God shed his grace on thee,
> And crown thy good with brotherhood
> From sea to shining sea!

The famous images so eloquently conjured up in our mind by this song are part of our collective national identity—but it was not always so. In 1804, when the Corps of Discovery set out, it was by no means an established truth that this sweeping mosaic of natural beauty was our country's future.

Before the Corps of Discovery journeyed westward, no American citizen had laid eyes on the spacious skies over Montana, witnessed the boundless expanse of amber waves of grain swaying in the wind across the plains of North Dakota, or absorbed the breathtaking beauty of the Rockies' "purple mountain majesties." It was Lewis and Clark and the Corps of Discovery who were the first Americans to see and describe these emblems of America. They were also the first Americans to bestride the continent from coast to coast. That is, they were the first to fully comprehend— and experience—the term "from sea to shining sea." That we can now do it in four hours in the comfort of an airliner at 35,000 feet only makes Lewis and Clark's two-and-a-half-year pilgrimage across the country that much more impressive.

The Corps of Discovery was also the first official exploration of unknown spaces commissioned by the United States government.[5] Its legacy lives on to this day in the spirit of the men and women who work for NASA. And as the *Challenger* and *Columbia* tragedies remind us, the risks associated with exploration are high. Lewis and Clark are the forefathers of this proud heritage.

But Lewis and Clark did more than just explore new spaces; they documented and recorded copious amounts of information to share with mankind. They described hundreds of different plants and animals. In this sense, their spirit of exploration and quest for knowledge is no different from those of the pioneers who are today exploring the uncharted regions of the ocean, the human body, and even the human mind and sharing their findings with mankind. Lewis and

Clark serve to remind us that we have an obligation to advance knowledge and, in Lewis's words, "relieve distressed humanity."

The journey of the Corps of Discovery is integral to America for another important reason: It was a continuation of the "American Experiment" started in 1776. Thomas Jefferson—the same man responsible for penning what has become the foundation of America with these immortal words: "We hold these truths to be self-evident, that all men are created equal, that they are endowed by their Creator with certain unalienable Rights, that among these are Life, Liberty, and the pursuit of Happiness"— also wrote the following:

> [I]t is impossible not to look forward to distant times, when our own rapid multiplication will expand itself beyond those limits and cover the whole . . . continent, with a people speaking the same language, governed in similar forms and by similar laws.

It was Lewis and Clark who took the first step in turning Jefferson's vision into a reality. It was they who first documented and secured the land that allowed our democracy to blossom. Before Lewis and Clark, the western boundary of America was at St. Louis, and the immense tract of land that Thomas Jefferson had purchased from France in the Louisiana Purchase was an unknown commodity. The journey of the Corps of Discovery changed all of this. Bernard DeVoto, editor of *The Journals of Lewis and Clark*, wrote that their journey "was the first report on the West, on the United States over the hill and beyond the sunset, on the province of the American future." As the first "westerning" pioneers, Lewis and Clark gave the country a direction, lit the torch of America's westward expansion, and instilled in Americans a sense of infinite possibilities.

Firing the American Spirit

But even more than the physical accomplishments of discovering and documenting the land that gave shape to America, Lewis and Clark epitomized—and helped create—the enduring American spirit. They did not just establish the future westward direction of America; they forever cemented our identity as a bold, peaceful, freedom-loving, and forward-moving people. If the physical movement of the Corps of Discovery helped establish the natural boundaries of the American Experiment, their human interactions expanded the spiritual boundaries of our freedom.

The core American principles of equality and democracy were ever-present throughout the expedition. From their unusual arrangement to share command to their willingness to select men only on the basis of merit and, most especially, their visionary decision to grant every person—including Sacagawea, the young Indian woman, and York, Clark's black slave—the right to vote on an important issue, the captains represented the best of the American spirit.

As Dayton Duncan said in Ken Burns's documentary, *Lewis and Clark: The Journey of the Corps of Discovery*, "Lewis and Clark at their best is America at its best." In this sense, Lewis and Clark shed light not only on who we are as a country and what we have become, but, more important, on who we can yet still become.

THE JOURNEY OF THE CORPS OF DISCOVERY

A Summary of Key Events and Dates

Preparations

On **January 18, 1803,** President Thomas Jefferson requested a $2,500 authorization from Congress to fund an exploration of the Missouri River to the Pacific Ocean. The request, and its subsequent approval, officially initiated the Journey of the Corps of Discovery.

Throughout the spring of 1803, Meriwether Lewis prepared for the journey. He traveled to Philadelphia and studied botany, celestial navigation, and medicine, seeking out some of the day's top experts. In June, perhaps sensing that the expedition was beyond the scope of any one person, Lewis invited William Clark, a friend and a former commanding officer of his, to join him on the expedition. As part of the offer, Lewis agreed to share command.

On **July 4, 1803,** the same day that the historic Louisiana Purchase was officially announced to the nation, Meriwether Lewis departed from Washington, D.C. As he ventured west, Lewis spent the better part of the summer purchasing supplies and overseeing the construction of a fifty-five-foot keelboat that would carry many of the men and the supplies up the first leg of the Missouri River to the Mandan Indian villages. During this period, Lewis and Clark had also begun assessing and hiring some of the first men who were to accompany them on their journey.

On **October 14, 1803,** Lewis and Clark were officially reunited and together continued down the Ohio River until they reached their winter camp, Camp Dubois, which was located near the confluence of the Mississippi and Missouri rivers. The two captains spent the winter months hiring and training more men, gathering supplies, and collecting as much information as they could about what lay to the west. It was during this period that the Secretary of War, Henry Dearborn, refused to honor Lewis's request that William Clark be granted a rank equal to his own. Lewis informed Clark that he would abide by their earlier agreement to share leadership, and no one ever knew that Clark was anything but Lewis's equal.

In **March 1804,** Lewis and Clark, for the first time, disciplined some of their men for disobeying orders, fighting, and getting drunk. They approached each matter fairly and attempted to prevent repeat incidents by clearly establishing the rules and by administering mild punishments in the form of confinement to camp and extra labor.

The First Leg of the Journey:
Up the Missouri to Fort Mandan

On **May 14, 1804,** Lewis and Clark and approximately forty-eight men, including twelve French boatmen (also called engagés), departed from Camp Dubois. The members of what would become the permanent party—those members who would make the entire journey—boarded the keelboat in order to begin cultivating an atmosphere of teamwork and esprit de corps, while the others rode upriver in two pirogues (i.e., large canoes).

Two days into the journey, the captains were still building their team. On **May 16, 1804,** the captains added Pierre Cruzatte and Francis Labiche, both of whom were half French and half Omaha Indian.

The following day, **May 17, 1804,** Lewis and Clark conducted their first court martial. Three men were sentenced to receive lashes for being AWOL. It was the first use of corporal punishment and served as a reminder to all that they were on a military expedition and were now officially in a "war zone."

Throughout the remainder of the spring and summer, the Corps of Discovery made slow progress up the powerful Missouri River. On **August 20, 1804,** the Corps of Discovery suffered their only casuality of the entire expedition when Sergeant Charles Floyd died of a burst appendix. Shortly thereafter, Lewis and Clark took the unusual step of holding an election to replace Floyd. Patrick Gass was elected by his peers and approved by the captains.

This same month, Moses Reed, a private in the Corps of Discovery, attempted to desert but was caught, court martialed, punished, and permanently disbanded from the party. Later that fall, a second member was also disbanded from the party for mutinous behavior.

On **September 25, 1804,** the Corps of Discovery encountered one of its tensest moments when the Partisan, a Teton Sioux chieftain, threatened to halt the expedition's progress upriver. The Partisan was not satisfied with the trade goods he had received and wanted more. The captains refused to give in to his demands and were prepared to fight if necessary. Both sides were poised for a violent battle when the situation was defused by another Sioux chieftain, who ordered that the Americans be allowed to proceed.

Having safely navigated past the Teton Sioux, the Corps of Discovery arrived at the Mandan villages on **October 26, 1804,** and eventually established camp at Fort Mandan, near present-day Bismarck, North Dakota. The captains used the winter months to gather intelligence, record all of their findings for a report to President Jefferson, and prepare their men for the next stage of the journey. It was during this period that Lewis and Clark added Toussaint Charbonneau and his wife, Sacagawea, to the permanent party to act as interpreters. On **February 11, 1805,** Sacagawea gave birth to a baby boy, Jean Baptiste. He was known as "Pomp."

The Second Leg of the Journey: Into Unknown Territory

On **April 7, 1805,** the Corps of Discovery departed Fort Mandan and entered unknown territory for the first time. Lewis wrote on this day that he was "most confident" in succeeding and that the Corps of Discovery was in "perfect harmony." For the next two months, the expedition made slow but steady progress across what is today eastern and central Montana. Along the way, they had a few encounters with grizzly bears and on another occasion almost lost one of their boats—along with all of its supplies—to a strong sudden wind. The boat and supplies were saved only because of the quick actions of Pierre Cruzatte and Sacagawea.

The next challenge occurred on **June 3, 1805.** On this date, the captains were confronted with a fork in the river and had no idea which branch represented the true Missouri. Lewis and Clark analyzed the situation, reviewed all of their intelligence, and spent a number of days exploring each fork. Even though every member of the party was convinced the northern fork was the Missouri, the two captains thought otherwise, and they selected the southern fork. Their decision proved correct, and on **June 13, 1805,** Meriwether Lewis first reached the Great Falls of Montana. For the next month, Lewis and Clark and their team completed a brutal eighteen-mile, thirty-two-day portage that tested the limits of their physical endurance. The unexpected delay caused the Corps of Discovery to lose valuable time. With the summer days now getting shorter and the Rocky Mountains still to the west, Lewis and Clark were nervous about their prospects for reaching the Pacific before winter set in. They needed to locate the Shoshone Indians, on whom they were depending to provide horses that were essential to successfully crossing the mountains.

On **August 12, 1805,** Meriwether Lewis peered over the Continental Divide, becoming the first American to do so. He discovered that, unlike what he had expected, there was no westward-flowing river within portaging distance. In fact, there were only more mountains—mountains as far as the eye could behold. The need to quickly locate the Shoshone became more desperate. Luckily, the very next day, Lewis spotted some Shoshone Indians. The captains were able to successfully negotiate for horses and, despite some tense moments in which the Shoshone questioned the Corps of Discovery's friendly intentions, also solicited the

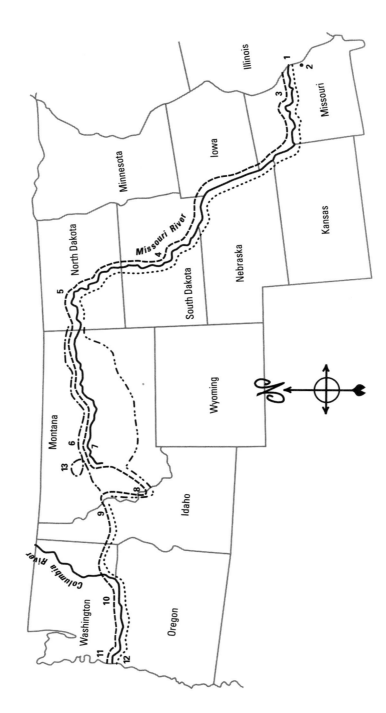

Route of the Lewis and Clark Expedition

——————— Route of outward journey (1804–1805)

················ Return trip together through Oregon and Idaho (1805)

——————— Return of Lewis (through Montana)

··—··—··—·· Return of Clark (through Montana)

················ Return together down Missouri River (1806)

1. Camp Dubois: The site of the Corps of Discovery's 1803–1804 winter camp.

2. St. Louis: A city of approximately 3,000 residents in 1804.

3. Sergeant Floyd's grave: The site of the burial place of the only Corps of Discovery member to die during the 28-month expedition.

4. Confrontation with the Teton Sioux: The site where the Teton Sioux threatened to halt the expedition. The captains narrowly avoided a deadly battle.

5. Fort Mandan: The site of the Corps of Discovery's 1804–1805 winter camp.

6. The Decision at the Marias: The confluence of the Marias and Missouri rivers. The captains did not know which river was the Missouri, but after a thorough investigation, they ultimately chose the correct river.

7. Great Falls of the Missouri: The location of an 18-mile, 32-day portage around five different waterfalls.

8. The Continental Divide: Meriwether Lewis expected to find another river on the other side, but he only saw more mountains.

9. The Bitterroots: The location of a brutal 12-day trek across rugged mountainous terrain.

10. The Columbia River: A dangerous stretch of river which included numerous violent rapids.

11. The Pacific Coast: The site of the historic vote in which all the members of the Corps of Discovery, including Sacagawea and York, were allowed to vote on the location of their winter camp.

12. Fort Clatsop: Winter camp 1805–1806.

13. Confrontation with the Blackfeet Indians: The site of the Corps of Discovery's only deadly encounter with Indians. Meriwether Lewis and a small group killed two Blackfeet tribesmen.

Shoshone's assistance in helping them portage their equipment for a part of the journey.

On **September 11, 1805,** having hired "Old Toby," an Indian guide, to help them, Lewis and Clark courageously began crossing the Bitterroot Mountains. For twelve harrowing days, the Corps of Discovery braved cold, wet, and snowy weather and treacherous conditions. Exhausted and hungry, they finally emerged on the other side on **September 22, 1805,** where they were greeted by the Nez Percé Indians. The Nez Percé tribe graciously befriended them, provided food, and helped them prepare for the next stage of their journey.

The Third Leg of the Journey: West to the Sea

For the better part of **October 1805,** Lewis and Clark and their team confidently tackled a series of violent rapids on the Columbia River as they continued westward. By early November, they had reached the Columbia Estuary (which they mistakenly thought was the Pacific Ocean), and on November 7, 1805, William Clark wrote his immortal passage: "Ocian in view! O! the joy."

Later that same month, on **November 24, 1805,** after being pinned down for more than a week by rain and wind, Lewis and Clark made their historic decision to allow everyone—including York, the black slave, and Sacagawea, the teenage Indian woman—to vote on the location of their winter camp. It represented the first truly democratic vote by an American group. Two weeks later, in adherence with the vote, Lewis and Clark officially established Fort Clatsop.

The Corps of Discovery remained at Fort Clatsop until **March 26, 1806,** when they began the first leg of their return trip. By early May, the Corps of Discovery had reached the Nez Percé's camp. For the remainder of the month and well into June, the expedition patiently bided their time while they waited for the snow to recede so they could recross the Bitterroots.

The Return Journey: Recrossing the Continent

On **June 10, 1806,** the captains started their trip back over the Bitterroots. A week later, the conditions proved so horrendous that for the only time in their journey, Lewis and Clark ordered a "retrograde" march and they returned to camp. After waiting an additional week and deciding to hire some local Indian guides, the Corps of Discovery successfully recrossed the Bitterroots.

On **July 3, 1806,** in order to conduct an exploration of those territories they did not cover on their initial westward trip, Lewis and Clark agreed to split up. Lewis explored the northern area, including the Marias River, while Clark and a small party surveyed the Yellowstone River. In late July, while still exploring the Marias, Lewis encountered a small group of Blackfeet Indians, and on **July 27, 1806,** the expedition had its only deadly encounter with Indians. Lewis and one of his men killed two Blackfeet warriors who attempted to steal some rifles and horses. To escape danger, Lewis and his party rode their horses for more than twenty-four hours (and covered nearly 100 miles) until they were successfully reconnected with other members of the expedition.

Ironically, Lewis survived his close call with the Blackfeet only to be shot on **August 12, 1806,** by one of his own men, who mistakenly thought he was an elk. In mid-August, the entire permanent party of the Corps of Discovery was briefly reunited, then on **August 15, 1806,** John Colter, a valuable member of the Corps of Discovery, who would later go on to discover what is today Yellowstone National Park, was granted permission to leave the party and returned to the wilderness with two other traders, and on **August 17, 1806,** the Corps of Discovery bid farewell to Charbonneau and Sacagawea.

For the remainder of August and for the first three weeks of September, the Corps of Discovery quickly traveled downriver and, after 863 days traveling more than 8,000 miles, the Corps of Discovery successfully returned to St. Louis on **September 23, 1806.**

PART TWO

✣ ✣ ✣

The Leadership Principles
of Lewis and Clark

CHAPTER ONE

PASSIONATE PURPOSE

The Principle of a Higher Calling

By adverting to the dignity of this higher calling, our ancestors have turned a savage wilderness into a glorious empire, and have made the most extensive and the only honorable conquests not by destroying, but by promoting the wealth, the number, the happiness of the human race.

—Edmund Burke

Twelve years before Lewis and Clark reached the Pacific, Alexander Mackenzie, a Scottish explorer working as an agent for the North West Company (a fur-trading company operating under the auspices of Great Britain), made a daring transcontinental journey across Canada and, on a rock located near Bella Coola, British Columbia, penned the famous line: "Alexander Mackenzie, from Canada, by land, the twenty-second of July, one thousand seven hundred and ninety-three." In so doing, he became the first European to make a land passage across the North American continent. By 1801, a full three years before Lewis and Clark's party even got under way, Mackenzie had published a book about his expedition entitled *Voyages from Montreal.*

Why, then, one might ask, do we celebrate Lewis and Clark and not Alexander Mackenzie? It is a fair question. Mackenzie is certainly worthy of both praise and historical attention, but there are three reasons why his accomplishments are surpassed by those of Lewis and Clark.

First, Mackenzie's trek to the Pacific was done entirely for commercial purposes. Acting as a private agent, Mackenzie's goal was to locate an all-water route in order to further the fur-trading interests of the British Empire. In fact, his book begins with a general history of the fur trade and concludes with a call to the British Parliament to place commerce in the pelts of beaver and sea otter under the control of private Canadian fur traders.[1] Lewis and Clark's voyage of discovery, by contrast, was much broader in concept. It was dedicated to nation building, the Manifest Destiny of the United States to expand to the Pacific, land exploration, scientific and cultural discovery, and commercial trade.

The second reason Lewis and Clark receive greater attention than Mackenzie is because their expedition went deeper in the execution of its mission. Mackenzie recorded few scientific findings on plants or animals and provided little useful information on the indigenous peoples he encountered. In his book, Mackenzie admitted as much by stating, "I do not possess the science of a naturalist," and noting that he didn't have time to "collect the plants which nature might have scattered on the way." In short, his journey did little to extend the knowledge of the human race. As noted by Lewis and Clark historian James Ronda, Alexander Mackenzie "wore but one hat."

Compare this with Lewis and Clark, who left behind, through their journals, one and a half million words about everything—from the land, animals, and Indians they encountered to the flora, fauna, fish, and fossils they found. They chronicled a virtual treasure trove of scientific and cultural information for the entire civilized world to digest. In their day, Lewis's surveys on the Indians represented the first glimpse of those peoples and cultures, and Clark's maps served as invaluable guides to the first generation of explorers who helped settle the American West.

All told, Lewis and Clark recorded more than 200 plants and animals that were new to science and noted at least seventy-two different Indian tribes.[2] But in order to fully comprehend the depth of the captains' contribution to society, it is important to understand that their writings still offer value today. Lewis's documentation of certain Indian tribes—which are now extinct—remains the sole source of information society has on these cultures, and his recordings of various plants and weather conditions still provide present-day botanists and meteorologists useful historical information.

The third, and most important, reason that Lewis and Clark stand apart from Alexander Mackenzie as historical figures, however, is because of their commitment to a higher purpose. As men of the Enlightenment, Meriwether Lewis and William Clark wanted to leave their mark on the world by expanding the base of human knowledge; and, as patriots, they wanted to further the cause of liberty by extending the great American Experiment of democracy to the recently purchased Louisiana Territory and beyond to the Pacific. Their commitment to these higher purposes, which transcended the mere worldly aspirations of power, glory, ego, or money, shines through their journals, and it is clear they affected virtually every action and decision Lewis and Clark made.

It is therefore with this first leadership principle, passionate purpose—the principle of a higher calling—that I begin Part II of this book.

Men of the Enlightenment

To begin to understand Meriwether Lewis and William Clark, it is necessary to understand that they were both products of eighteenth-century Virginia; and Virginia, at that time, is where the American Enlightenment most flourished. This meant that from an early age, both men were steeped in the philosophy of the Enlightenment.

Meriwether Lewis best espoused the philosophy in his journal entry of August 18, 1805:

> This day I completed my thirty first year, and conceived that I had in all human probability now existed about half the period which I am to remain in this Sublunary world. I reflected that I had yet done but little, very little indeed, to further the happiness of the human race, or to advance the information of the succeeding generation . . . and resolve in the future . . . to live for *mankind,* as I have heretofore lived *for myself.*

In this single passage, Lewis tells us almost everything we need to know about why Thomas Jefferson had chosen him to lead the expedition and why he decided to accept the invitation. He wanted to contribute something of real and long-lasting value to society. He wanted to make the world a better place.

In his book *William Clark: Jeffersonian Man on the Frontier,* Jerome Steffen correctly pointed out that "Clark never wrote anything like 'I am an Enlightenment man.'" But Steffen added that it became "apparent through his actions that [Clark was] saying 'My life was deeply affected by Enlightenment ideas and Jeffersonian principles.'" William Clark, like Meriwether Lewis, understood from the beginning that the journey was about more than commerce.

The key tenets of the Enlightenment philosophy shed valuable light on how Lewis and Clark, by embracing the philosophy, unwittingly prepared themselves for the expedition and how it influenced their respective decisions to accept the invitation to co-lead the expedition.

The Enlightenment held that "progress . . . was a product of individuals seeking to uncover the secrets of the universe."[3] From this perspective, then, the very nature of the expedition—an invitation to travel into and discover the unknown—spoke to the very purpose of their being. More than just an intellectual opportunity, the invitation to explore the interior of the North American continent was a calling to a higher purpose and makes Lewis and Clark's decision to leave their comfortable lives and their loved ones behind easier to understand.

Another tenet of Enlightenment thinking held that man was rational and, through education and training, had the potential to do good. Lifelong education, therefore, was an essential prerequisite to giving meaning to one's life, which helps explain why both men placed so much emphasis on educating themselves and on acquiring skills to "uncover the secrets of the universe."

Finally, the Enlightenment held that spiritual fulfillment was obtained by seeking God's natural order through the application of the natural sciences and constant observation. The expedition, Lewis and Clark knew, would call forth both responsibilities in spades and thus represented an opportunity for spiritual fulfillment. William Clark captured this sentiment when he wrote that his religious duties included "endeavoring to make our fellow creatures happy." He believed that the new knowledge the Corps of Discovery would discover could, in some measure, bring happiness to his fellow man. Lewis, while arguably less spiritual than Clark, picked up on this theme when he said, after the expedition returned in the fall of 1806, that one of the purposes of the expedition was to "relieve distressed humanity."

Children of the American Revolution

This enlightened thinking, which also manifests itself in the writings of America's founding fathers—and thus in the very creation of America itself—also necessitated that the country and the principles upon which it was founded be protected. Born in 1770 and 1774, respectively, Clark and Lewis grew up literally and figuratively in the shadow of the Revolutionary War. William Clark's oldest brother, George Rogers Clark, was a hero of the Revolutionary War and helped secure the Ohio and Kentucky frontiers from British-sponsored Indian invasions. So significant were his accomplishments that Benjamin Franklin once said of the elder Clark, "Young man, you have given an empire to the Republic." Eighteen years his junior, William Clark grew up hearing stories from his older brother and was greatly influenced by him. The fact that four of his other brothers fought in the war—including one who died a prisoner on a British warship— also had a lifelong impact on him. At his first opportunity, Clark followed them into the military.

Meriwether Lewis, whose family motto, *Omni solum forti patria est*, can be translated as "Everything the brave man does is for his country,"[4] was similarly influenced by his family. His birth father, William Lewis, served without pay as a lieutenant under George

Washington, as did his stepfather, John Marks, who served as a captain in the Army.

In 1794, Lewis joined the Army to help suppress the Whiskey Rebellion, a revolt by people living in the West who were opposed to the federal government taxing their whiskey. Unsympathetic to the rebels' cause, Lewis wrote that he joined the Army "to support the glorious cause of liberty, and my country." It is a phrase that he repeated in later correspondence to his family.

A Decision to Lead

In 1803, like two rivers converging, "Enlightenment opportunity" merged with patriotic necessity. At the time, the entire territory west of the Mississippi embodied the great unknown. Therefore, to men of the Enlightenment, it represented the opportunity to advance human knowledge. It was also one of the primary reasons Jefferson felt compelled to explore the uncharted regions.

Then in July 1803, as the expedition was still in its preparation phase, the United States purchased from France the Louisiana Territory. The country doubled in size overnight. The U.S. government needed to understand what it had just purchased and required a small team to explore this new land and report back on both the opportunities and the challenges that the new territory represented.

Furthermore, the territory to the west of the Louisiana Territory, the Oregon Territory, was still up for grabs in the high-stakes game of international politics. Great Britain had already begun to lay a claim to the entire territory after Alexander Mackenzie's successful land crossing through Canada in 1793 and George Vancouver's naval expedition to the Northwest the previous year. Thomas Jefferson understood that the United States had to act fast. Lewis and Clark also realized what was at stake, and it stirred their patriotic fervor to be able to serve their country by beating the British to the territory and securing the area for their country and countrymen.

Balance of Personal Interest with the Common Good

Little is known about Lewis and Clark's personal motivations to co-lead the expedition, but it is realistic to assume that neither man did it entirely for altruistic purposes. Lewis's journal entry on April 7, 1805, in which he compared the expedition to "those deservedly famed adventurers," Christopher Columbus and James Cook, suggests that he was very cognizant of the potential for future fame. That both men would be entitled to land grants in excess of 1,600 acres upon the successful completion of the journey cannot be discounted as a source of motivation, nor is it unreasonable to assume that William Clark, as the younger brother of a legendary war hero, joined the expedition as a way to measure up to his older brother's accomplishments.

However, none of these factors alone explain why the two took on all the risks associated with the transcontinental journey. For example, if Lewis had aspired solely to power, he would have chosen to remain the personal secretary to the president of the United States, where, by day, he could move among society's most powerful politicians and, by night, dine with many of the world's greatest thinkers. Instead, he willingly left his high-powered position in the White House for a life of hardship, danger, and uncertain success. Moreover, if Lewis had been interested solely in glory, he would have chosen to lead the expedition by himself, without the assistance of William Clark. If the expedition had been about ego, William Clark would never have agreed to share command with a man four years his junior who had once served under Clark's command. And if either man had been interested in money, they would have been far better off managing and adding land to their vast plantations—something both men were extremely capable of doing.

Instead, Lewis and Clark sought to align their own self-interest with the national interest and the greater good of mankind. The Age of Enlightenment philosophy held that this was not only possible, but actually desirable. As Jerome Steffen noted, "The trip to the Northwest made sense to William Clark—not just for himself but for the good of the country."

It is important to understand that Lewis and Clark did not first seek fame, power, and riches with the idea that those tools would then be used to benefit their country and mankind; it was the other way around. By advancing knowledge for mankind and fostering liberty, they were confident that they would also personally benefit.

For instance, once they had reached the Pacific Ocean, fame was undoubtedly theirs, but rather than hasten their return to St. Louis to bask in their newfound celebrity, the captains knowingly prolonged their journey and agreed to split up on the return trip in order to explore more of the Louisiana Territory. Their respective trips yielded little information that would be of personal benefit to either man, but they understood that their maps of these new areas would greatly help those who would follow.

Lewis and Clark both planned to profit from their knowledge of the fur-trading business (the most profitable industry of the day) upon their return. Yet, instead of focusing exclusively on the fur trade, as Mackenzie did, they spent considerable time reporting on the mineral composition of the soil. They were as interested in addressing the question of whether the land was suitable for their fellow countrymen for future agricultural development as they were in furthering their own personal interests.

The aforementioned examples are illustrative of the fact that Lewis and Clark always kept the higher purpose of their mission at the forefront of their actions.

The Foundation

Lewis and Clark's purpose of advancing knowledge for the benefit of mankind and securing liberty for the benefit of their countrymen, while never officially written in any mission statement, created the foundation upon which the edifice of the entire expedition rested. Upon his return, Meriwether Lewis captured the sentiment of this commitment when he emphasized that the worthiness of the expedition was "the merit of having added to the world of science, and of liberty . . ." It is therefore important to take a moment to understand how this higher purpose affected their other decisions.

Chapter Two will review their historic decision to share leadership. Because their personal goals were not driven by power, glory, or ego, Lewis was able to select William Clark as his co-commander and make him "equal in every respect," and Clark was willing to accept this offer. Without a higher purpose, such decisions would be unlikely.

Chapter Three will assess their extraordinary skill in preparing for the journey. The fact that the purpose of their journey transcended mere personal rewards undoubtedly helped focus their attention and provided the rationale for acquiring the best equipment and spending the time necessary to do things just right.

Chapter Four will discuss how Lewis and Clark embraced diversity. Without first understanding what the Enlightenment philosophy says about individuals advancing on the basis of merit alone, it is difficult to comprehend the captains' actions. Men of higher-class society applied to accompany the expedition but were turned away because Lewis and Clark were only interested in finding the most qualified individuals. If the mission had only been about money, they might well have allowed a few family friends to share in the opportunity.

Chapter Five will explore the captains' unique approach to discipline and their willingness to inflict severe punishment at times and remain flexible at others. It is clear that their commitment to a higher purpose—and not mere adherence to a set of rules—guided their actions.

Chapter Six will discuss Lewis and Clark's willingness to personally exercise leadership at the most dangerous moments of the expedition. Their commitment to a higher purpose dictated that responsibility could not be delegated and demanded that they "lead from the front."

Chapter Seven will review Lewis and Clark's willingness to learn from others. They knew their responsibilities transcended those of just explorers, and they therefore needed to spend considerable time and effort learning new subjects and enhancing and updating their skills. If they had been interested solely in commercial gain, it is unlikely they would have reached out to so many people and learned so many new skills.

Chapter Eight will consider Lewis and Clark's unrelenting optimism. Their positive outlook stemmed in part from a belief that the purpose of their mission was so noble and important that they simply could not afford to ponder the consequences of failure.

Chapter Nine will look at Lewis and Clark's approach to risk. Only by first considering their true motives can their penchant for—and their willingness to accept—risk be understood.

And last, Chapter Ten will reflect on how Lewis and Clark cultivated a true sense of team spirit. To a great degree, the glue that bonded the Corps of Discovery was the captains' commitment to a higher calling.

Several of the chapters will touch on the relations the co-commanders forged with the Indians. The Enlightenment stressed that all mankind evolved from one universal body and differed only in stages of development. This idea clearly influenced Lewis and Clark's ability not to deal with the Indians as "savages"—as most of their countrymen viewed them at the time—but instead to acknowledge them and treat them as individuals worthy of respect. If the captains had only been interested in exploration, they might have taken a wholly different—and decidedly more negative—approach toward dealing with the Indians. Instead, to a great extent, they treated the Indians hospitably, with fairness and dignity.

Even many of the lesser decisions the captains made must also be placed within the deeper context of their commitment to a higher purpose. For instance, Lewis and Clark were willing to forge ahead during their brutal thirty-two-day portage around the Great Falls and their nearly fatal eleven-day ordeal in the Bitterroot Range because the stakes were higher than just commercial interests.

As military commanders, they were under no obligation to solicit, let alone listen to, the opinions of their men. Yet they did. To the extent that their men had opinions on whom they wanted to replace Sergeant Charles Floyd (the sole expedition member to die during the journey), which fork in the river was the Missouri (a crucial decision point reached in June 1805, with the men convinced it was north while the captains believed it was south), and where to set up camp in the winter of 1805–1806, Lewis and

Clark wanted to know those opinions because something far greater than money, power, or glory was at stake.

Finally, their commitment to a higher purpose shielded them against disappointment when they failed in their primary goal of finding a "practical all-water route" to the Pacific. Their higher purpose allowed them to press on with the knowledge that they still possessed useful information that would interest mankind and benefit their fellow countrymen. It is why Clark continued to toil over the drafting of new maps and Lewis diligently recorded all the ethnographical information about the Indians long after they determined the fabled Northwest Passage was nonexistent.

Leading Into the Unknown

Lewis and Clark are not unique in their commitment to a higher purpose. In fact, it appears almost to be a recipe for success. Among the great innovators and businessmen of the past two centuries, there is one common thread that unites them all and that is a belief that business is something more than just making a profit. This sentiment was best captured by Henry Ford when he said, "A business that makes nothing but money is a poor kind of business."

Robert Fulton, an inventor and contemporary of Lewis and Clark, did not set out to invent the steam engine. Rather, as an ardent free trader, Fulton saw trade as the great liberator of people, and he was concerned that the growing power of foreign navies could threaten trade—and thus liberty—by establishing blockades and imposing taxes and levies. He therefore set about not to invent "something" but instead to find a way "to destroy such engines of power." He started with the broad goal of protecting trade and advancing liberty, and it was only his unrelenting focus on this issue that led him to develop the steam engine. The process might seem backward to many, but to a man of the Enlightenment, as Fulton was, it made perfect sense.

Samuel Morse, inventor of the telegraph, and Alexander Graham Bell, inventor of the telephone, were similarly motivated. Each man wanted to help the public communicate better. They persisted in promoting their technologies for this reason and because they believed their devices also held great strategic military value to the United States.

The legacy continued in the twentieth century and was perhaps best epitomized by Bill Hewlett and David Packard, the founders of Hewlett-Packard Company. In their simple words, "HP exists to invent the useful and the significant." The term *useful*, they believed, was important because, if achieved, it would allow their customers to pursue more rewarding endeavors. By *significant*, they meant products that not only made a profit but made a difference. This clear mission guided the company, which grew from a small start-up operating out of a garage in California to the one of the largest corporations in the world.

It would be unrealistic, however, to assume that every businessperson needs "to make the world a better place" in as significant a manner as Fulton, Morse, Bell, Ford, or even Hewlett and Packard. Lewis and Clark's principle of "passionate purpose" holds a number of practical lessons for today's executives and forms a solid foundation for doing business well into the future.

Start with a higher purpose. "To live for mankind" and "to relieve distressed humanity" were not just throwaway phrases for Meriwether Lewis—in the way many companies' mission statements are today. The phrases provided real guidance to the Corps of Discovery. A present-day corporation that operates successfully under a similar model of committing to a higher purpose is Medtronic, Inc., a multinational manufacturer of medical devices located in Minneapolis, Minnesota. In 1960, with his fledgling company on the brink of bankruptcy, Earl Bakken, then-CEO of Medtronic, sat down and wrote a mission statement for his company. It started with the phrase "To contribute to human welfare" and ended with "To maintain good citizenship as a company." Bakken was not content to simply post this mission statement in the lobby of the company headquarters and forget about it. To demonstrate the human aspect of his company's mission, every December for the company holiday party, Bakken would bring in six patients, along with their families and physicians, to tell Medtronic employees how their lives were improved by Medtronic products.

William George, who replaced Bakken as CEO and chairman in 1989, recounted the story of how in the early 1990s an executive committee recommended that he sell the company's drug administration system. Medtronic had lost $25 million over ten years developing this system. Then, before a buyer could be found, George met a young man at a Medtronic holiday party who was born with spastic cerebral palsy. From the time the young man was three years old until he was sixteen, he had to undergo a surgery every summer to relieve the spasticity of his muscles. The procedure, which involved the selective cutting of sensory nerves, would leave him confined to a body cast for eight weeks. Eventually, a new drug was found to treat the disease, and it was administered through the drug system that Medtronic was hoping to divest. The boy told George how the drug and Medtronic's drug-delivery system had changed his life because he no longer had to spend his summer in a body cast and awoke every morning feeling great.

George decided then and there not to sell the system. As he said, "A purely economic decision would have said 'kill this business.'

A human decision, on the other hand, said 'Here's a device that can save or impact hundreds of thousands of lives.'" Under George's tenure, the business not only became profitable, it became one of Medtronic's most significant businesses.[5]

By adhering to Bakken's original mission and basing his decisions on higher principles, George grew Medtronic's revenues from $750 million to $5 billion and enhanced its market value from $1 billion to $60 billion during his tenure. He did so with the philosophy that "[t]he real bottom line of the corporation is not earnings per share, but service to humankind."

A smaller company operating under the same principle is Adaptive Eyecare, Ltd., a small private start-up based in England. In the mid-1990s, Joshua Silver began working with Estée Lauder to develop an inexpensive mirror that users could adjust to magnify their own reflections. His goal, he said, was to make "piles of money." During his research he realized that he could adjust the focus of the glass lenses. Immediately, he set aside work on the mirror and began developing cheap adjustable eyeglasses because he recognized his discovery could eliminate the need for eye exams and the costly infrastructure of a lens-grinding facility and thus bring corrected vision to an enormous number of people in the Third World.[6] Although it is too early to tell if Silver and his company will succeed, prospects look promising.

Medtronic and Adaptive Eyecare are not unique in the business world. From insurance companies to cosmetic companies, businesses are staying competitive and profitable by committing to purposes that transcend money and employing other lessons of Lewis and Clark's "passionate purpose."

Put customers first, self second. As officers in the Army and as agents of the United States government, Lewis and Clark were really working for their fellow citizens. In this sense, the citizens were their customers. Their actions demonstrated that they never forgot this fact. On every step of the expedition, they always took the extra effort to diligently record new information, or explore and document new areas for the benefit of those who would follow after them. In short, they were always thinking of their customer first.

A company that operates under the same principle is Northwestern Mutual. Under Jim Ericson's management from 1993 to 2001, Northwestern Mutual operated with one simple rule: Do whatever is in the customer's interest. This rule was manifested in an extraordinary form in the late 1990s when one customer's life insurance application for his new daughter was delayed because the baby's doctor hadn't sent in proper information to document the policy; when a Northwestern Mutual agent called to explain the delay, the father informed the company that his baby had died of sudden infant death syndrome. Northwestern Mutual, which was under no obligation to honor the policy because it was not yet approved, instead chose to honor the policy because the client had done everything that was required of him. Perhaps even more telling is that Ericson didn't even know of this decision until after it had been completed because employees knew how Ericson wanted them to act.[7] The company demonstrated that this was not a one-time event. In the wake of the 2001 terrorist attacks, Northwestern Mutual quickly instituted a policy of paying life insurance claims to the families of victims even without a death certificate because it best served their customers.

Put country before profit. As mentioned previously, fur trading was among the most profitable industries of Lewis and Clark's era, and both men, upon their return, became involved in the industry. There is no indication, however, that they ever placed their own personal interests above those of their country. William George, the former CEO of Medtronic, tells another story of meeting Dennis Kozlowski, the former CEO of Tyco International, in 1998 to discuss a possible acquisition. Shortly before the meeting, *Business Week* had named Kozlowski one of the top twenty-five managers of the year and placed him on the cover of the magazine. At the meeting, Kozlowski bragged that by having its headquarters in Bermuda, Tyco was able to avoid paying U.S. taxes. George immediately left the meeting and canceled all further talks with Tyco—even though this was not in Medtronic's financial interest. George simply didn't want to do business with anyone unpatriotic or unethical. (Kozlowski was later charged with looting $600 million from the company and, along with the executives of Enron and Global Crossing, became one of the poster boys for corporate malfeasance.)

Align personal interests with the common good. Doing what is right is not incompatible with making money. The fact is that William Clark did profit from his experience (and Meriwether Lewis likely would have—had he not died shortly after the expedition in 1809). Both Medtronic and Northwestern Mutual continue to be very successful, as are a number of other businesses that have learned to align their financial interests with the common good. A good example is Mary Kay Ash, founder of Mary Kay Cosmetics. She started her company in 1963 not to get rich, but rather because she wanted to provide women with an opportunity for personal and financial success. Jim Stowers, founder of American Century, a mutual fund, has a similar story. He started the fund not to get wealthy but because he wanted to help people become financially independent.

These stories may appear to be just isolated incidents, but in 2002, Curtis Verschoor, a professor at DePaul University, conducted a study on whether socially responsible behavior pays off. He reviewed the overall financial performance of *Business Ethics* magazine's 100 Best Corporate Citizens and compared their performance against the remaining companies in the S&P 500. What he found was that on the basis of sales growth, profit, and return on equity, the socially responsible companies were "ten percentile points higher."

Proceed On!

On September 11, 2001, Howard Lutnick, CEO of Cantor Fitzgerald, lost 700 of 1,000 employees at the World Trade Center. On "Larry King Live" a few months after the tragedy, the host pointed out how in one brief moment Lutnick had changed from a street-fighting, win-at-all-costs, bottom-line-driven CEO to something completely different. In response, Lutnick replied, "How could I not change?"[8]

It is a statement that everyone can understand and empathize with, and my point is not to unfairly criticize Lutnick, but rather ask this deeper question: Should one's thinking have to change in light of a tragedy?

Lewis and Clark were extremely fortunate that only one man died on the expedition. However, had more—or even all—perished from disease, a losing battle with Mother Nature, or a deadly fight with Indians, it is difficult to think that either Lewis or Clark would have uttered a similar line. The captains knew they were pursuing a worthy purpose. As a result, their actions had a clarity and consistency that transcended the short-lived goals of money, power, and fame and provided a strong foundation for everything they did. They could not have changed because to have done so would have been to diminish the odds of success of their mission.

In the end, Lewis and Clark's commitment to a higher purpose was not a "luxury." It was essential to the expedition's success. Their commitment to a higher purpose helped optimism prevail over pessimism, curiosity over arrogance, compassion over callousness, and risk taking over comfort. It strengthened the captains' resolve during times of danger, helped stave off defeatism when defeat seemed imminent, and served as a constant motivating force to themselves and the Corps of Discovery throughout the expedition.

By committing to a higher purpose, you too can do the same.

CHAPTER TWO

PRODUCTIVE PARTNERING
The Principle of Shared Leadership

*When we see men of worth, we should think
of equaling them . . .*
—Confucius

It is one of the most famous invitations to greatness in the history of exploration. On June 19, 1803, Meriwether Lewis wrote a letter to his friend and former commanding officer, William Clark, inviting Clark to join him on his journey to explore the interior of the North American continent. It read, in part:

Thus my friend, you have a summary view of the plan, the means and the objects of this expedition. If therefore there is anything under those circumstances, in this enterprise, which would induce you to participate with me in it's fatiegues, it's dangers and it's honor's, believe me there is no man on earth with whom I should feel equal pleasure in sharing them as with yourself.

But what is truly interesting is that earlier in the letter, Lewis had offered Clark a most unusual arrangement. The short phrase— it is but nineteen words—could have been the most important Meriwether Lewis ever wrote. He informed William Clark, "Your situation if joined with me in this mission will in all respects be precisely such as my own."

To what extent Lewis's offer of shared leadership influenced Clark's decision is not known, but there can be little doubt it made the decision that much easier. Nearly six weeks after Lewis wrote him, Clark received the letter (mail moved no faster than a horse at the beginning of the nineteenth century) and responded on July 29, 1803:

The enterprise &c. is such as I have long anticipated and am much pleased with, and as my situation in life will admit of my absence the length of time necessary to accomplish such an undertaking I will cheerfully join you in an "official char- rector" as mentioned in your letter, and partake of the dan- gers, difficulties, and fatigues, and I anticipate the honors & rewards of the result of such an enterprise . . . My friend I do assure you that no man lives with whom I would prefer to undertake Such a Trip &c. as yourself.

The men's early correspondence lays the foundation for their second leadership principle, productive partnering, or the princi- ple of shared leadership.

Co-Command

The very concept of co-command or shared leadership runs counter to almost every principle of military and business leadership. And at the turn of the nineteenth century, when rank consciousness was nearly born into every Virginian, the idea was even more foreign. As Meriwether Lewis's biographer, Richard Dillon, once noted, it was "like putting two scorpions in the same bottle."

Neither Meriwether Lewis, William Clark, nor Thomas Jefferson ever elaborated on why the decision of shared leadership was made, and yet it is clear the decision was made early in the planning process. Some have speculated that the demanding nature of the mission—with its extraordinary responsibilities for recording findings, managing men, and dealing with Indians, all while under constant threat of death from illness, accident, or war—dictated that the unconventional structure be put in place. Others have suggested that Meriwether Lewis was acutely aware of his own shortcomings and understood that the success of the mission required that he shore up his deficiencies with someone who complemented his own skills.

The truth likely incorporates aspects of both theories. Neither, however, explains why Lewis selected William Clark specifically. It is known that while Lewis anxiously waited for Clark's response to his historic invitation, he also approached Lieutenant Moses Hooke, a competent and talented Army officer, about accompanying the expedition. There is no indication, however, that Lewis ever considered offering Hooke a rank equal to his own. It was William Clark that Meriwether Lewis most wanted, and he was willing to give his former commanding officer a stature equal to his own in order to entice him.

The decision reflects very well on Meriwether Lewis. Given the competitiveness of exploration and the glory that would accompany a successful mission, no one would have criticized Lewis for assuming sole command of the expedition. Instead, he set aside his own personal interests and selected a man of incredible strength—a man whose talents in many areas exceeded his own. Lewis chose a man of great character who, by virtue of his former relationship with him, would not be afraid to question tactics, challenge strategy, or express his opinion. In short, Meriwether Lewis wanted a man who could help the mission succeed, not a "yes man." He found all of that and more in William Clark.

Respect

From the first letter, when Lewis wrote that "there is no man on earth with whom" he would want to share the responsibilities of the expedition more than Clark, to when Clark responded "no man lives with whom I would prefer to undertake Such a Trip . . . as yourself," it was clear that in spite of their different personalities and temperaments, both men genuinely liked and respected each other. This respect served as the foundation of their effective partnership.

From early in the journey, when they were still on the Ohio River and Clark fell ill and Lewis cared for his companion, to the very end, when Clark comforted Lewis after he had been accidentally shot by one of his men, examples of their friendship and affection are plentiful.

So great was their respect for one another that the closest to a disagreement that was recorded over the course of the 863-day, 8,000-mile journey is when Clark refused to comment on Lewis's ill-fated iron boat experiment in his journal. Fearing there would be limited materials from which to construct canoes, Lewis ordered an elaborate collapsible iron frame, built in Harper's Ferry, and had it hauled up the Missouri. When covered with animal skins, it was estimated it could haul 8,000 pounds. Stephen Ambrose and others have interpreted Clark's unusual silence (he rarely mentioned the project during the twelve days that the iron-framed boat was being constructed) as his gentlemanly way of expressing his displeasure over the time and effort expended on the project.[1]

All in all, it is not much to go on and hardly reflects the stuff of a great rift. The incident is, however, illustrative of another important component of shared leadership, which is that decisions, even if they are not unanimous, must appear to be. Never is there the slightest indication that Clark expressed any doubt about the iron boat to the others in the party, nor is there any mention in their journals of any other disagreement between the captains throughout the entire expedition.

Trust

The second tenet of an effective partnership is trust. In his first letter, Lewis wrote that Clark's "situation . . . will in all respects be precisely such as my own." However, during the winter of 1803, Meriwether Lewis was notified by the Secretary of War, Henry Dearborn, that due to the peacetime reductions in the military, Clark could only be offered a lieutenancy—not the rank of captain. Lewis was mortified. It was not what he had told Clark, and it is not what President Jefferson had approved. (Why Jefferson didn't involve himself in this situation is unknown.) Lewis vehemently objected to Dearborn, but to no avail. Lewis immediately wrote Clark: "It is not such as I wished or had reason to expect but such as it is . . . I think it will be best to let none of the party or any other persons know about the grade, you will observe that the grade has no effect upon your compensation, which by G-d, shall be equal to my own."

True to his word, Lewis never referred to Clark as anything other than "captain," and there is no evidence that Lewis ever pulled rank on Clark or that any of the party ever knew of the slight (which was corrected by an act of Congress in November 2000, when it posthumously conferred upon William Clark the rank of Captain in the Army).

Moreover, well after the expedition, Lewis remained true to his word and continued to fight for equal compensation for Clark. In a letter to Dearborn in 1807, Lewis implored the secretary "that there should be no distinction in rank." In the end, Lewis was able to secure an equal land grant for Clark, but not the agreed-upon rank or the corresponding compensation. The issue, however, never became public and Clark was always referred to as captain.

To Clark's immense credit, although miffed at the slight by Dearborn, he simply stated to Lewis that the mission came first. When asked by Nicholas Biddle, the first person to edit Lewis and Clark's journals, to explain their relationship, Clark simply responded: "Equal in every respect." And, by all accounts, they were just that: equal in every respect.

Complementary Skills

Dead reckoning was an essential navigational skill for the pilots of riverboats at the beginning of the nineteenth century. The skill was used to plot a boat's course and chart its progress upriver. The skill was also valuable because, in the hands of an experienced practioner, it could be used to draw accurate maps. By all accounts, William Clark was the more capable of the two leaders in this area. Meriwether Lewis, on the other hand, was the more seasoned celestial navigator, skilled in using the stars to determine the longitude and latitude of a particular location.

I start with this practical distinction because it succinctly captures the different personalities of the two captains. Clark was the more tactical of the two, better at handling the day-to-day affairs. Meriwether Lewis was more the visionary and strategic thinker. He was able to conceptualize the big picture.

Using the standard of today's Myers-Briggs test, Lewis was clearly the more introverted and Clark the more extroverted. Lewis was more "thinking" and Clark more "feeling." Lewis was more "judging" and Clark more "perceiving." There are fewer distinctions in the "sensing and intuitive" area. Of the two, Lewis was more mercurial and Clark the more mild-mannered partner.

These different personality traits allowed the captains to communicate and interact with the members of the expedition in different and deeper ways. Lewis was known for taking long, lonely walks that helped refresh his sense of purpose and imbued him with a genuine optimism that was based on his understanding of the big picture, whereas Clark's day-to-day interaction with the men, along with his positive "can do" attitude, was a vital ingredient in helping the Corps of Discovery overcome the myriad of obstacles that threatened to derail the expedition.

Lewis's "thinking" approach was helpful when it was necessary to coldly calculate the realities of a particular difficult situation. For instance, when the men were past the point of exhaustion in the Bitterroot Mountains and surviving on nothing more than candles and colt meat, it was Lewis who led them forward. Clark, by nature of his more easygoing and extroverted personality, was more popular with the men. During the long winter months when boredom could easily have given way to disciplinary problems (and sometimes did), Clark would organize shooting parties to hone the men's shooting skills and then reward the winner with either a small monetary prize or an extra dram of whiskey. And when morale was dipping and the troops needed some positive reinforcement, it was more often than not Clark who provided it.

Lewis and Clark also brought to bear different skills in their relations with the Indians.

Meriwether Lewis seemed to demonstrate a more effective psychological understanding of the Indians. On at least two occasions he applied his understanding of the Indian psyche to the benefit of the expedition. In August 1805, with fall and cooler weather quickly approaching and with the party still on the eastern side of the Rockies, the expedition needed to rely on the Shoshone Indians for horses to portage over the mountains. The Shoshone, who had been ambushed by neighboring tribes in the past, were wary of being led into a trap. Lewis had to convince them to stay. First, he tried telling them that the white man did not lie. (This was something of a stretch—as later American actions would attest—but in Lewis and Clark's case it was true, with minor exceptions.) Next, he implied that if they would not cooperate, the Americans would withhold trade from the tribe in the future. And when that proved ineffective, Lewis challenged the Indians' courage and manhood by saying, "I still hoped that there were some among [you] . . . not afraid to die." As Lewis recounted in his journal, he found that he had touched the "right string; to doubt the bravery of a savage is at once to put him on his metal." A few days later, after still not connecting with the rest of his party, whom he said were coming upriver, the Shoshone again began to doubt the sincerity of Lewis; in fact, some tribe members were convinced he was leading them into an ambush by a warring Indian tribe. Lewis again resorted to his understanding of the situation and offered the Indian chief his gun and ordered his men to similarly hand over their guns to the other Indian warriors as a sign of trust. The act worked and confidence was restored. Shortly thereafter, Lewis was reunited with Clark and a full trust had been established with the Shoshone.

Clark was equally skilled with the Indians, albeit in a different capacity. Clark appears to have been the more artful negotiator. He truly respected and liked Indians, more so than Lewis, who, on occasion, had some harsh comments about Indians in his journal entries.

Clark's calm temperament and respect for Indians eased the expedition through some very difficult times. One poignant example occurred on the return trip when a band of Chinook Indians stole Lewis's faithful Newfoundland dog, Seaman. Although the dog was quickly recovered, soon thereafter an Indian stole some other equipment from the party. The normally cool Lewis flew into a rage that far exceeded the situation and he threatened to "birn every house" if the Indians didn't return the stolen items. The Indian chief, alarmed that Lewis would threaten his entire village over the actions of a single person, quickly denounced the threat. What happened next is not well documented, but William Clark was apparently able to calm his friend and appease the Indian chief.

It is interesting to note that the one episode of violence, which happened when Lewis and a small group encountered the Blackfeet Indians in July 1806, occurred when the captains had separated for the return trip across the continent. Whether Clark could have prevented the tragedy, in which two Blackfeet Indians died, will never be known. What is known is that Clark prevented the previously mentioned potentially explosive situation and was an effective counterbalance to Meriwether Lewis.

Lewis and Clark's differences transcended what today might be referred to as "soft skills." Both men brought unique, tangible skills to the expedition. Lewis was the better botanist and was more comfortable on land. Clark was a superior cartographer and the more skilled boatman. As military officers, both men were trained medical practitioners, but Lewis was the better-trained doctor, although Clark had a more human touch with patients. On the return trip, when the Nez Percé Indians sought medical treatment for minor ailments, they turned to Clark.

These practical differences allowed each man to concentrate his strengths on those areas where they could add the most value. Clark's ability to more quickly guide the keelboat upriver meant precious time was saved, which allowed him more time to explore the numerous streams and creeks that littered the landscape, which meant he could draw more accurate maps. And, as Clark was manning the keelboat, Lewis was on land discovering and documenting new plants and animals. The arrangement also gave Lewis more time to conduct celestial navigation and thus determine their location. This information, in turn, helped place Clark's detailed maps in their proper strategic location and greatly aided the next generation of American explorers. It is therefore the perfect illustration of how the two complemented each other and, together, were greater than the sum of their individual parts.

The Benefits of Two

By default or design, the fact that there were two officers also ensured that twice the amount of work got done. At the beginning of the journey, before they even left Camp Dubois, Lewis went to St. Louis and rounded up the necessary provisions while Clark stayed behind and built the winter camp, constructed the keelboat, trained the men, and oversaw the trial runs up the Mississippi River. The fact that Lewis and Clark were equal in rank ensured that when one man made a decision—especially in the absence of the other—it was final. There was no concern among the enlisted men that the other captain would overturn it.

Two supervisors also meant that hunting parties were better organized, equipment was repaired quicker, and the daily chores—such as making camp, repairing clothes, and building canoes—were completed on time because at least one of the officers was always present to oversee the completion of those activities. Furthermore, when one got sick, the other ensured that everything stayed on task. So beneficial was having two leaders that after one near fatal accident in which a pirogue almost capsized—and neither Lewis nor Clark was aboard—the captains vowed never to leave the boat unless the other was present.

A Confidant

In June 1805, when the captains were confronted with their fateful decision at the Marias River (concerning which fork represented the true Missouri) and Lewis had finished his exploration of the north fork and Clark had completed his trip up the south fork, the two leaders returned to camp and conferred in the privacy of their tents. They were aware that the members of the party were adamant in their belief that the north fork represented the true Missouri. The fact that the two captains had each other to confide in certainly played a role in their willingness to go against the opinions of everyone in the group, including the expedition's master boatman, and select the other (but ultimately correct), southern course of the river. By double-checking their facts with each other, probing the other's thinking for flaws, acting as a sounding board for each other's thoughts and doubts, and then reaching a consensus decision because they were "equal in all respects," the captains achieved two very important things. One, their decisions were strengthened by the rigors of their partner's cross-examination and, two, their confidence in their decisions was fortified because they had been confirmed by the other. This confidence, in turn, went a long way toward bolstering morale and building trust in the captains' future decisions.

As Lewis noted in his journal after he and Clark had announced their decision to follow the southern fork, everyone went along "cheerfully"—even though they still disagreed with the decision.

Leapfrogging Captains

The third benefit of Lewis and Clark's sharing leadership responsibilities, in addition to getting more work done and bringing different skills to the table, was that the two were able to split up on occasion and leapfrog each other. The decision at the Marias River, where Lewis searched up the north fork and Clark the south, is again a good example. However, there were four additional times when the captains split up. The first occurred immediately after the decision at the Marias. To appease the men's concerns that they were following the wrong river, the captains agreed to send Lewis ahead to determine if their decision was the correct one. If it wasn't, then Lewis would return immediately in order to correct the decision as quickly as possible.

Upon reaching the Great Falls, which confirmed they were on the Missouri, shortly thereafter, Clark went out ahead and surveyed the route and found the quickest path to portage. While he did so, Lewis stayed behind and prepared the party for the portage. A month later, as the captains grew nervous at the prospect of finding the Shoshone Indians, Lewis ventured ahead to expedite finding the Indians. When the Shoshone informed the captains that the Salmon River was not navigable, Clark went ahead to view the situation for himself.

Even during their difficult trek across the Bitterroots, the captains split up. This time it was because the men's morale was dangerously low and they were on the brink of starvation. Clark and a small party went ahead in search of flat land and food. They set up camp and rounded up some meager provisions, which they then sent back to the rest of the party. Finally, on the return trip, Lewis and Clark split up again to explore more territory. Lewis documented the Marias River and Clark the Yellowstone River.

In every instance, the decision to split up produced fruitful results by saving time, increasing morale, or yielding valuable new information.

Leading Into the Unknown

At a time when the world is getting more complicated every day, the amount of information grows daily, and the introduction of new technologies threatens to overwhelm many businesses, the benefit of having a true partner is more obvious than ever. All of these factors make Lewis and Clark's example of shared leadership extremely relevant. A review of the characteristics that made their partnership work is instructive for today's business executives.

Equality in Word and Deed. Lewis and Clark really were, in Clark's famous phrase, "equal in every respect." That none of the men ever knew of Clark's lower rank is proof that Lewis adhered to this principle. The captains' actions stand in quiet contrast to many of the recent examples of co-leadership that have ended in failure. BankAmerica, Pharmacia, BP Amoco, Citigroup, and

DaimlerChrysler have all tried co-CEO arrangements in the last few years and failed. The reason they failed is because for co-command to work, it must be real in both word and deed. In most cases, one of the co-CEOs actually held more power in the arrangement.

This is not to say that shared leadership can't work. A present-day illustration of an effective co-CEO relationship is that of John Addison and Rick Williams at Primerica Financial Services, an Atlanta-based subsidiary of Citigroup, which has more than 100,000 independent sales agents and annual revenues of nearly $2 billion. The arrangement between the two has been in place since 1999 and allows each man to focus on his strengths, while not being overwhelmed by the complexities and significant responsibilities of the job.

Trust. Both Lewis and Clark knew the other man's word was his bond. In 1803, after learning of Dearborn's decision, Lewis wrote Clark that his rank would "by G-d" be the same as his own. Four years later, Lewis was still fighting to rectify the matter and appealed again to Dearborn to give Clark his due rank and pay. Contrast this with the DaimlerChrysler example. At the time of the merger, Robert Eaton, CEO of Chrysler, and Juergen Schrempp, CEO of Daimler-Benz, held a press conference and announced that they intended to be not only co-CEOs but co-equals in every sense. The arrangement lasted a little over a year until Eaton left the company. Schrempp later admitted that he never viewed the situation as one of co-equals.

Mutual Respect. From the start, when Clark accepted Lewis's offer to join the expedition by writing, "My friend I do assure you that no man lives with whom I would prefer to undertake Such a Trip," to the very end, when Lewis was fighting for equal pay and compensation for William Clark, it is clear that the two men had a great deal of respect for each other. Without respect, a productive partnership is not possible.

One such example can be found in the partnership of George W. Bush and Dick Cheney. In the spring and summer of election year 2000, George Bush was fighting a losing public relations battle that portrayed him as lacking the gravitas and the foreign policy experience to handle the presidency. Shedding the time-honored tradition of choosing a running mate who offered "geographical balance," Bush instead selected Cheney. Cheney was a man Bush had admired and respected from the time Cheney served in his father's cabinet as the head of the Defense Department. In spite of his similarities with Bush (both were from the West and had ties to the oil industry), Cheney was also a well-respected Washington insider who had served as chief of staff to President Gerald Ford and had spent over a decade in Congress before being tapped to be secretary of defense. In making the selection, Bush knowingly brought a more seasoned person onto the ticket. Cheney had everything that the younger Bush lacked. Yet rather than wallow in insecurity, Bush disregarded Cheney's own advice on whom he should select for vice president (Cheney, ironically, had headed up Bush's screening committee for the position) and chose him. The decision was comparable to Lewis's selecting the more senior and more experienced military commander to accompany him on his journey. Bush understood that he wasn't just selecting a "yes man"; he was selecting someone who would openly challenge and question his decisions. And Cheney's decision to serve with a younger and arguably less qualified man, like Clark's decision, indicated that the respect was mutual. He understood Bush possessed skills that he lacked. Of course, because the presidency can't be shared, the analogy falls short. However, George W. Bush's decision stands in quiet contrast to his father's selection of Dan Quayle for vice president.

Different Skills. The partnership of Lewis and Clark worked in large measure because each man added real value. As noted earlier, Lewis was the better botanist, zoologist, and doctor. Clark was the better boatman and cartographer, and he had more rapport with the men. Their skills compensated for deficiencies in the other and allowed each to concentrate his efforts where they were most effective. In the case of Primerica, one CEO, Addison, oversees the sales and marketing departments while the other, Williams, runs the administration and finance departments. Each man plays to his respective strengths and thus frees the other up to concentrate more time and energy on other important functions.

Common Experiences. Both Lewis and Clark were military officers with years of experience on the frontier. As such, they shared common experiences and could communicate with each other based on those experiences. They were both also entrepreneurial and comfortable with assessing and taking risks, and the daily rigors of the expedition required flexibility and an ability to handle ambiguity. Without these similar tendencies, it is unlikely the partnership would have functioned as well. Their shared philosophical outlook helped ensure that each understood where the other man was coming from at all times.

Using the example of Primerica once again, another reason the partnership works is because Addison and Williams, in addition to having different skills, have both spent the better part of their careers working for the company. As such, they share a common experience that allows each to understand the other better and helps them avoid problems arising from philosophical differences or miscommunication.

Communication. Little is recorded of Lewis and Clark's daily conversations, but, as officers on the frontier, they undoubtedly debriefed each other on an almost daily basis. Not only did this allow them to share information, but they could also use the opportunity to review decisions in an environment free of outside intervention. The process helped to improve their decisions and bolstered the captains' confidence in those decisions. For any partnership to work, communication must be frequent and honest.

United Front. It was almost inevitable over the course of the 8,000-mile journey that the captains had differences of opinion on various issues, yet never once was there any indication that their decisions were anything but unanimous. In every partnership, there are going to be disagreements, but how those issues are resolved matters greatly. For shared leadership to work, disagreements can—and must—be aired privately. However, once a decision has been made, the "public" face of that decision must be unanimous.

Proceed On!

The Commission on Public Trust and Private Enterprise, which was established to review corporate governance in the wake of the Enron, Tyco, and Global Crossing corporate scandals, has renewed the call for companies to separate their CEO and chairman positions. Moreover, a recent survey of family businesses found that 13 percent already have co-CEOs and that, in the future, 35 percent of those surveyed felt that they would move to a co-CEO relationship. The two findings suggest that shared leadership is only going to become more common in the future. Lewis and Clark, by their example, show that not only can shared leadership work, it can actually enhance the prospects for success for virtually any venture.

For twenty-eight months, through unbelievably harsh conditions and trying circumstances, Lewis and Clark handled every situation masterfully. The fact that there were few emergencies is a testament to their leadership skills. This success did not, however, arise out of simple good fortune. It happened because Meriwether Lewis made a conscious decision to fully share leadership responsibilities with William Clark. As a result, the expedition benefited by having a deeper reservoir of talent and skills to draw upon. There were two minds reviewing every decision, two bodies sharing the tremendous workload, and two sets of eyes recording all the expedition's valuable findings. The arrangement clearly worked for Lewis and Clark, and it can work for business leaders who are willing to make the effort.

CHAPTER THREE

FUTURE THINK
The Principle of Strategic Preparation

Plans are nothing; planning is everything.
—General Dwight Eisenhower

Before leaving on their expedition, Lewis and Clark's knowledge of the interior of the continent was so fuzzy they believed it plausible that they might find massive volcanoes, mountains of pure salt, and prehistoric mastodons on their journey. They even believed they might find the mythical lost tribe of Welsh Indians (a group of Welshmen who allegedly reached America in the 11th century and, when their boat sank, stayed as an English-speaking white tribe).

It is easy to make light of these things today, but in 1803 there was no body of knowledge that could contradict these hypotheses. Yet it was upon this state of knowledge (or lack of it) that Lewis and Clark had to prepare for a journey in which they did not how long they would be gone or how serious the threats and challenges would be; and they had only the vaguest notion of what skills, supplies, and equipment would be most useful.

It was a difficult task, to say the least, and yet, to their immense credit, Lewis and Clark ran out of only three items—tobacco, whiskey, and Indian trade goods. The items that they absolutely could not afford to run short of—guns and ammunition for hunting and personal safety; paper and ink for their journals; and boats for transportation—were well provided.

Lewis and Clark also did an extraordinary job on the smaller things. In fact, so meticulous was their planning that when they ran out of candles on January 20, 1806, the captains were prepared because they had had enough prescience to pack extra wicks and some candle molds to manufacture their own candles (for wax they resourcefully relied on elk fat). Because of their foresight, Lewis and Clark had candlelight by which to continue writing in their journals and drafting maps well into the long winter nights during the remainder of their stay at Fort Clatsop, their camp during the winter of 1805–1806. I recount this seemingly insignificant story because it is an illustration of Lewis and Clark's third leadership principle, future think: the principle of strategic preparation.

The captains' planning success can be attributed to the five unique aspects of strategic preparation: meticulous preplanning, acquisition of the best equipment, extraordinary attention to detail, a focus on efficiency, and thoughtful long-term planning.

Preplanning

Lewis and Clark's journey, although spurred to a large degree by Thomas Jefferson's reading of Alexander Mackenzie's account of his expedition through Canada to the Pacific, was not a hastily arranged expedition. Thomas Jefferson had been thinking of such an expedition since at least 1783. As a result, Jefferson had contemplated to a significant degree what such a journey might entail. Meriwether Lewis, as Jefferson's personal secretary, undoubtedly had lengthy conversations about the topic with his mentor. Furthermore, both men scoured the writings of Mackenzie and others looking for clues about what the expedition might encounter. We know, at a minimum, that in addition to Mackenzie's book, Lewis also read George Vancouver's book, *Voyage of Discovery to the North Pacific Ocean*, and was knowledgeable about the experiences of various traders such as David Thompson, an agent of the North West Company whose map of the region (up to the Mandan villages) was the most detailed of the day. In fact, Lewis made a hand copy of this map to accompany him on the trip.

The captains' due diligence yielded three very important findings. First, as a result of Vancouver's trip to the Pacific Northwest, Lewis and Clark knew where the continent ended. This allowed them to figure that "as a crow flies," the North American continent was roughly 3,000 miles in length. What neither Vancouver nor any other person could tell them was how far west the Missouri River flowed, where the Columbia River started, what the distance between the two rivers was, and, most important, what the land in between the Mandan villages and the Pacific Ocean held in store.

The second item that the co-commanders learned from their advance work was the approximate location of the Mandan villages, the largest known Indian village and the site where Lewis and Clark intended to make camp during the winter of 1804–1805. According to Thompson's maps, Clark concluded that the journey from Camp Dubois (their starting point) to the Mandan villages would be 1,500 miles. He was very close. The ultimate distance was 1,600 miles. This information provided Lewis and Clark enough knowledge to at least reasonably plan the first leg of the journey.

Third, from Thompson's experiences (as well as those of other traders), Lewis and Clark learned what trade items the Indians would find of value. Of the original $2,500 that Congress earmarked for the expedition, $667, or more than 25 percent (the single largest budget item), was dedicated to Indian trade goods. The list may appear to be arbitrary to the untrained eye, but Lewis's diligence proved extremely useful because in doing his homework, he came to understand that blue beads were considered of greater value than red or white beads by the Indians and that vermilion paint was highly coveted because it symbolized "peace." This latter fact proved useful when the Corps of Discovery encountered the Shoshone Indians for the first time in the summer of 1805 and members of the expedition were able to paint the faces of three Indian women with the vermilion-colored paint. The act signaled to the male warriors (who arrived shortly thereafter) that the party came in peace and may have been instrumental to the Corps of Discovery's survival.

The Best Equipment

Meriwether Lewis and William Clark knew that to a large extent the success of the expedition rested on the party's ability to both acquire their own food and, if necessary, protect themselves against hostile Indians and wild animals, such as grizzly bears. Therefore, guns were their most valuable resource. As a result, Meriwether Lewis was determined to get the best. In his day, the best was the Harper's Ferry model 1803 rifle, a .54-caliber flintlock rifle. The quality was such that Secretary of War Henry Dearborn would later make the rifle standard Army issue. Lewis purchased fifteen. He also commissioned one of the finest blacksmiths of his day to build a powderless air rifle. The rifle, which had a compression chamber in its stock, was often fired with great ceremony by the captains to impress the Indians. The rifle was meant to symbolize the promise of what American trade could bring to the Indians—in the form of weapons and advanced technology—if they entered into a trade agreement with the United States.

Next to guns, the expedition's next most prized possessions were its boats. The most important was the expedition's keelboat, a fifty-five-foot wooden structure that carried them up the Missouri River on the first stage of the trip to the Mandan villages. Lewis commissioned a boat maker in Pittsburgh to build the boat and had expected it to be done by July 20, 1803. Ultimately, it was not completed until the end of August, and the Ohio River was running shallower by the day. Although frustrated almost to the point of abandoning the project, Lewis bided his time as the boat maker, who was often drunk, slowly completed the project.

As a result of the delay, the expedition was not able to travel up even a portion of the Missouri River in the fall of 1803—a fact that quite possibly delayed the Corps of Discovery's journey by a whole year. Once they did get under way, however, the boat withstood the intense forces of the Missouri River and served them admirably. By all accounts, the keelboat was an integral part of the expedition's success. A boat of lesser quality might well have fallen apart under the river's unforgiving powers.

Lewis's patience in waiting for the boat to be satisfactorily completed was time well spent. Notwithstanding Lewis's acerbic writings about the drunkenness of the builder, it should be noted that in the late 1980s, it took a team of twelve volunteers, using power tools, no less, more than sixty days to build a replica of the boat.[2]

Another purchase of note—and one that has often been portrayed as one of the expedition's greatest failures—was Lewis's decision to procure a 176-pound iron-frame boat. Both Lewis and Clark had received enough intelligence to convince themselves that large portions of the land surrounding the upper Missouri River might consist of barren, treeless plains. If true, the expedition would not be able to build canoes and thus continue their journey up the river once the keelboat was no longer able to navigate the shallow waters. This thinking led Lewis to order the construction of an elaborate iron-frame boat capable of carrying four tons. Although some historians have criticized Lewis for his insistence on dragging the device 2,000 miles upriver, only to see it fail because of a lack of an adequate supply of pine tar to attach animal skins to the exterior of the frame, the criticism is inherently unfair. The fact that it did not work (and that they ultimately didn't need it) does not diminish the foresight Lewis demonstrated in planning for a contingency (the absence of trees) which, had it occurred, could have ended the expedition.

Even after the Corps of Discovery crossed the Bitterroot Mountains in September 1805 and were about to descend the wild waters of the Columbia River, the captains continued to insist on acquiring quality equipment. In this case, the best equipment was a Chinookan canoe. In Clark's words, "These canoes are neeter made than any I have Seen and Calculated to ride the waves and carry emence burthens." Lewis and Clark therefore bartered with the Chinooks and were able to acquire the canoe.

The final item that the captains did not skimp on was medicine. At one point in the preplanning phase, Lewis entertained the notion of bringing along a doctor. It was a reasonable consideration. After all, the probability of a large group of men traveling across thousands of miles of unfamiliar territory requiring medical treatment at some point during the journey was nearly inevitable. Yet, Lewis and Clark decided against it for two reasons. One, as military officers, their own skills as doctors were not sufficiently less than those of even the day's best trained doctors. Second, the rigors of the expedition would likely have meant that a skilled doctor unaccustomed to the daily burdens of frontier life would have created more problems than he solved. Lewis therefore did the next best thing and consulted with the preeminent doctor of his day, Benjamin Rush. With Rush's assistance, Lewis amassed an impressive list of medical supplies and drugs. Included in the expedition's medicine chest were mercury, opium, calomel, and Peruvian bark as well as thirty other drugs. Much of the medicine is now known to have been ineffective, if not altogether counterproductive. Still, the mercury, in spite of being toxic, probably served its purpose for treating venereal disease, and the Peruvian bark, it is believed, likely saved Sacagawea's life during her near-death illness in June 1805.

Although the medicine was not terribly effective, it demonstrated (as the iron-frame boat did) that Lewis and Clark anticipated the contingencies they might encounter and then proceeded to procure the best supplies known at the time to address these contingencies.

QUESTION EVERYONE

After Lewis and Clark descended the Ohio River in the fall of 1803 and made camp near St. Louis for the winter, they continued their meticulous preparations. Not content to idle away the winter, Lewis and Clark interviewed a number of individuals, including James Mackay, perhaps the most experienced Missouri River trader of his day. They even developed a comprehensive question-naire that was sent to individuals who might have useful knowl-edge of the Missouri River. So far-reaching was the survey that future president William Henry Harrison, then governor of the Territory of Indiana, received it and responded. All told, the cap-tains spent their time during the winter of 1803 wisely. Their efforts were extremely beneficial in identifying which Indian tribes they would encounter, where those tribes lived in relation to the river, and whether they were inclined to be friendly or hostile.

So comprehensive was their intelligence of the Indians that Lewis and Clark were able to premanufacture bundles of Indian trade goods in advance. Altogether there were twenty-one sepa-rate bundles; each was packed with great care according to the importance of the tribes and the various leaders they expected to meet en route to the Mandan villages.[1] This exercise helped ensure that they dispensed their trade goods in a manner that would not leave them short of trade items later in the journey.

Once the expedition began moving up the Missouri River, the captains' interrogations didn't stop. Every trader they ran across was queried. One trader, Pierre Dorion, who had suc-cessfully traded among the various Sioux tribes for years and was fluent in the language of the Sioux, was even persuaded to join their expedition.

In spite of the expedition's close call with the Teton Sioux in September 1804, in which the two parties nearly took up arms, Lewis and Clark's advance work paid handsome dividends as the Corps of Discovery successfully navigated the first stage of the trip to the Mandan villages.

Upon reaching their winter headquarters, the co-commanders redoubled their efforts and began interrogating scores of Hidatsa and Mandan Indians about the next stage of their journey.

Everything west of the Mandan villages was unknown to the Corps of Discovery, and the captains needed as much information as possible. From the Hidatsa, a tribe known for traveling widely, the captains learned the approximate location of the Great Falls, the Three Forks (a prominent landmark where three rivers converged), and the general vicinity of where the Shoshone were likely to be living. Lewis and Clark even put aside their disdain for the British and invited two British agents of the North West Company to come to their camp to exchange information.

By doing all this work, Lewis and Clark minimized their risk by obtaining as much information as possible and by learning the approximate location of key landmarks. As the co-commanders later found out, not every piece of intelligence they received from the Indians was accurate, although inaccuracy was the exception rather than the rule. The vast majority of the information was quite reliable and extremely beneficial. For example, although the Hidatsa did not alert the captains to the existence of the Marias River, they did inform Lewis and Clark that the Missouri River ran clear at the Great Falls. This seemingly small piece of intelligence helped Lewis and Clark overcome the objections of their men, who, at the fork in the river, argued that the Marias River was the true Missouri because it did not run clear.

Attention to Detail

Lewis and Clark, as a result of their vast experience on the frontier, had a rudimentary understanding of which items were bare necessities. They knew, for instance, that many of their dietary needs could only be met through hunting and thus ensured that the expedition had enough guns, ammunition, and, of course, the appropriate supplies to repair those guns. From experience, they also understood the importance of having compasses, sextants, telescopes, axes, saws, and carpentry tools. Like all good military commanders, Lewis and Clark also ensured that their men were adequately supplied with shirts, socks, coats, blankets, and the needles and thread necessary to repair and make anew those items.

But their preparation process went well beyond the basics. Before the expedition even got under way, Jefferson had developed a secret code that allowed the co-commanders to send important messages without fear of their being deciphered by enemy nations. The expedition's journals and the captains' correspondence to President Jefferson included a wealth of information that British, French, and Spanish traders—as well as their governments— would have found extremely valuable. And although there is no evidence to suggest that either Lewis or Clark ever employed the secret code, it is worthy of mention that the Spanish government, aided by General James Wilkinson, an American spy working on behalf of the Spaniards, did send out a small armed expedition in an effort to stop and imprison the Corps of Discovery. In the vast wilderness of the American West, the Spaniards never seriously came close to finding the Corps of Discovery, but the story serves as a reminder that the secret code might have been necessary. The fact that Lewis committed the code to memory is yet another demonstration of the extraordinary lengths to which the co-commanders went to prepare for various contingencies.

Lewis and Clark's attention to detail covered everything from Jew's harps, which were of considerable trading value with the Indians and helped add some musical diversity to the Corps of Discovery's nightly campfire entertainment session, to portable soup, for which Lewis spent $289—a staggering sum at the time. By all accounts, except by Lewis himself, the soup was universally despised. Still, it proved very useful during the harrowing journey over the Bitterroots, when the expedition was faced with near starvation, because it saved them from eating more of their horses than were absolutely necessary. (In spite of this, they were still forced to kill three colts for food.) If they had had to kill any more, it would have required that the supplies the horses were carrying either be carried by a member of the expedition or, more likely, simply be abandoned. And, at the time, less than halfway through the expedition, they were in no position to abandon any supplies.

The captains' attention to detail was not simply limited to physical items. Before departing from Camp Dubois, William Clark made the men load and unload the keelboat numerous times in an attempt to get it loaded just right. Too much weight in the bow, Clark knew, could cause the boat to get caught on a sandbar; too much weight in the stern would have made it vulnerable to a tree floating under the bow, which could cause it to capsize. In fact, almost immediately upon setting out on the Missouri, the keelboat was struck by a series of large uprooted trees, and had it not been for Clark's meticulous attention to this detail, the keelboat could have been lost.

The captains even included themselves in this preparation process. In November 1803, some six months before they set out, Lewis and Clark honed their surveying and dead-reckoning skills on the Mississippi and practiced their celestial navigation techniques. They wanted to make sure that when it really mattered, they did the job correctly.

Both leaders were also painfully meticulous when interviewing Indians and traders. To the men who had to serve as interpreters, the captains' obsession with asking the same question in slightly nuanced ways, as well as their need to ask the same question to a number of different people, must have seemed like an extraordinary waste of time. Yet, Lewis and Clark understood the importance of getting the information just right. For instance, the knowledge that the water "ran clear" at the Great Falls gave the captains valuable supporting information for selecting which fork represented the true Missouri River at a critical juncture. The decision saved the expedition valuable travel time which, had they followed the wrong river, could have proved fatal if they had had to cross the Bitterroot Mountains a few weeks later than they actually did.

Efficiency

A fourth component of Lewis and Clark's preparation success was their insistence on efficiency. If there was a better or more effective way of doing something, the co-commanders were always quick to embrace or adopt it. This thinking was best demonstrated by their decision to store their gunpowder in lead canisters. The decision, at first, might appear to add unnecessary weight to the expedition's already heavy cargo list. But when one considers that the expedition melted down the canisters after they were empty to make a new supply of bullets—and then recalls that the expedition never ran short of bullets—the decision makes a lot more sense.

Lewis and Clark demonstrated similar thinking in their decision to purchase a large oilcloth. The captains understood that not only could it be used to keep items dry, it could operate as a sail and help the expedition make better time up the Missouri River. Even the expedition's tomahawks doubled as peace pipes, so a party sent out to gather wood still had the necessary equipment—should they encounter Indians—to communicate their peaceful intentions.

The co-commanders were also shrewd enough to recognize in the winter of 1805, when they were running low on corn, that an old burned-out iron stove could be used to continue their trade with the Indians. Lewis and Clark ordered their black-smith to cut the stove into much smaller pieces and refashion the iron into valuable arrow tips for the Indians. The decision proved so successful that the Corps of Discovery had an ample supply of corn for the remainder of the winter. Once again, a seemingly small decision that might have easily been overlooked turned out to have large, positive implications for the success of the Corps of Discovery.

Forward Thinking

On three different occasions, Lewis and Clark decided to cache large amounts of food, equipment, and weapons in preparation for the return trip. At the confluence of the Marias and the Missouri rivers, at the Great Falls, and near the Three Forks they left behind items that were later recovered. In addition to refreshing the Corps of Discovery with supplies (most notably tobacco) on their return trip, the decisions also served to lighten their load by eliminating those items that were not of absolute importance.

At another point, after the Corps of Discovery crossed the Bitterroots, the party branded a number of horses and entrusted them to the care of Nez Percé Indians. Lewis and Clark knew that the horses were essential for a successful return trip but that they couldn't possibly take them down the Columbia. On their return trip, their trust in the Nez Percé was rewarded as they recovered a majority of their horses and used them to successfully recross the treacherous mountains.

Perhaps the best example of how Lewis and Clark were always thinking ahead was illustrated in their treatment of their journaling responsibilities. While their immediate goal was to find the most practical all-water route to the Pacific and lay claim to the land west of the Rockies for the United States, they never forgot that if they didn't make the return trip, all of their effort would be for naught. It was this thinking that led them to diligently record all of their findings from the first leg of the journey (from Camp Dubois to Fort Mandan) and then send those records back downriver with a small party in the spring of 1805. The report eventually reached President Jefferson in August 1805 and represented the first tangible return on his investment in the Corps of Discovery. The captains also copied portions of each other's journals to enhance the odds—should one get lost (an ever-present reality)—that at least one record of their valuable findings would survive.

Leading Into the Unknown

In spite of the two-century lag between Lewis and Clark's experiences and the challenges that confront today's business executives, there are still a striking number of parallels with modern business and some very tangible lessons for today's leaders.

Learn from and study others. Lewis and Clark were not the first Americans to try exploring the interior of the continent of North America. As recounted in Chapter One, they were not even the first to accomplish the goal. That distinction goes to Alexander Mackenzie. However, because Lewis and Clark were able to learn from Mackenzie as well as those others who went before them, they were able to succeed on a scale that surpassed Mackenzie. In this sense, Lewis and Clark were not significantly different from those companies that have come to market late, only to end up dominating it. For instance, Microsoft Corp. did not invent the Web browser, Federal Express was not the first priority air-freight service, and Procter & Gamble did not invent the disposable diaper; yet each company, by strategically assessing the market and learning from those that first entered the market, was able to become a market leader. They did it by learning the essentials, not repeating mistakes, and, where appropriate, incorporating new, improved ways of doing business.

Think long and hard about the future. Lewis and Clark conducted extensive research and consulted with a variety of people before departing on their expedition. This advance preparation helped them think through possible contingencies. Today's business leaders can do the same. There are any number of publications, books, or professional consultants dedicated to strategic planning, and while these resources may not be able to precisely predict the future, they can be useful in identifying new, emerging trends and positioning businesses to deal with—and profit from—these trends.

A good example of a company that does exhaustive planning is Royal Dutch/Shell. The company has a small twelve-person team called the scenario-planning group. Their function is to develop scenarios and alternative visions of the future based on broad demographic, technological, geopolitical, and environmental factors. Just as Lewis and Clark did, they engage in extensive research, consult with the experts, and contemplate the future with an eye toward meeting a wide range of different contingencies. The team has been in existence for more than thirty years and has had a number of successes. In 1972, the team developed a scenario called "Energy Crisis" that predicted a huge spike in oil prices. When the real crisis occurred the following year, Shell was the only oil company positioned to withstand the shock. A decade later, when prices collapsed, Shell was again prepared and spent $3.5 billion buying oil fields at depressed prices. The advance preparation has given the company a twenty-year price advantage over its competitors.[3]

In scenario planning, the team first identifies the company's primary goal. They then list all the micro factors that are relevant to that goal. Next, they identify the macro factors. Once this is done, they cross-rank the factors and the forces in terms of both their importance and their uncertainty. With this information in hand, they begin to flush out various scenarios and list the implications for their company if each were to occur. As a final step, they identify leading indicators that will signal if a particular scenario appears to be playing out. With this advance knowledge, the company can then take appropriate action to either prevent its marketplace position from eroding or, alternatively, enhance its position.

Allocate resources in advance. Lewis and Clark, by virtue of their due diligence, had a good idea of how many and which native tribes they would encounter on the first leg of their journey. As a result, they were able to allocate and budget their resources accordingly. This advance work ensured that they did not "over-trade" with any Indian tribes and deplete their resources early. In some ways, this is analogous to a new business that is just starting out and needs to manage its resources, particularly its cash. New businesses need to reach certain milestones (e.g., getting the product to market, profitability, etc.) and cannot afford to burn through their resources too quickly. By understanding the time frame in which these early milestones need to be reached, and by knowing approximately how many resources should be expended in reaching these goals, a business can constantly stay apprised of its situation and, if necessary, adjust its behavior accordingly.

Get the best equipment. Given an original budget of only $2,500, Lewis could have easily been tempted to save some money by purchasing lower-quality rifles or by forgoing the expenditures on medicine or portable soup, but he didn't. Instead, he bought the best equipment available and purchased the supplies and trade goods he felt were essential to the mission's success. The lesson for today's business executive is to not skimp on those few items where quality is absolutely essential. For instance, for some manufacturers, it may be the latest start-of-the-art equipment; for service companies, it may be personnel; and for still other businesses, it may be the physical location of the business. Regardless of what the "it" is, if it provides a significant competitive advantage, quality should not be sacrificed.

Focus on essentials. This is the corollary to the previous lesson. Although only appropriated $2,500 by Congress, Lewis and Clark were armed with an extraordinary letter of credit from Thomas Jefferson that allowed them almost unlimited purchasing power. They could have easily succumbed to purchasing items that were nice but not essential for the expedition's success (e.g., whiskey). Instead, the captains focused on essentials and did not run out of the few items that were absolutely vital to their success: guns and ammunition and paper and ink. Similarly, today's businesses often have access to liberal lines of credit. It can be easy, especially during the early stages of starting up a company, to overspend on office space, equipment, and furnishings. This tendency can be avoided by focusing only on those items that are essential for providing a strategic advantage.

Remember that some things can't be rushed. In the summer of 1803, Meriwether Lewis was anxious to set out, but he was stuck in Pittsburgh waiting for the keelboat to be completed. The Ohio River was running lower by the day, and he feared the expedition would lose an entire year if he could not get up the Missouri River at least partway. To his credit, he waited for the keelboat to be completed, and although he did lose valuable time, the keelboat served its purpose and safely transported the expedition up to the Mandan villages. Lewis's decision and the patience he demonstrated is analogous to a business waiting until a new product has been thoroughly tested before rushing to market. While it is possible that a slightly flawed product may suffice and may even be successful, the consequences of a failure must be weighed carefully. In Lewis's case, a failure in the keelboat would have proved extremely detrimental to the overall success of the mission, and he was wise to wait. In his case, there was no substitute for quality.

Focus on efficiency. A number of items served dual purposes on the expedition. For instance, depending on the weather, the oilcloth could be used either for sailing or for keeping items dry. Similarly, tomahawks were useful for either foraging or fighting. These dual-purpose devices provided the Corps of Discovery with increased flexibility to perform their daily chores. Today's corporations are entering an era where flexibility is becoming more important than ever. The question businesses need to ask themselves, based on Lewis and Clark's experience, is whether there are certain strategic resources that, if specifically manufactured, can serve dual or multiple purposes. Furthermore, just as Lewis and Clark reused the burned-out stove, businesses need to remain vigilant for opportunities where they can recycle, reuse, or resell components that have outlived a particular function.

Pay attention to detail. The captains did not have to practice loading and unloading the keelboat as many times as they did, nor did they have to bring extra supplies of vermilion paint and candle molds, or store gunpowder in lead canisters. Yet all of these small decisions proved very important. Analogies can be found in the need for today's businesses to retool their manufacturing operations, make special accommodations for foreign customers, keep extra supplies on hand, and utilize reusable packaging. Each factor alone may not make a big difference, but in total, they can add up to the difference between success and failure.

Leave things in reserve. Lewis and Clark's decision to cache items along the way served two purposes. First, in the few instances where they overestimated the amount of some items they would require, the caching allowed them to lighten their load. Second, and more important, they cached items that they either knew or believed they might need on their return trip. In many ways, the captains' decision was the equivalent of creating a rainy-day fund. For Lewis and Clark, weapons and ammunition were the "currency" of their day, and the lack of game to hunt would be comparable to economic slowdown. Therefore, they hedged against these possibilities by caching guns, ammunition, and dried pork. Businesses should also determine how many and what types of items they need to keep in reserve because of economic uncertainty and the possibility of external events over which they have no control.

Proceed On!

Before he even left Camp Dubois, William Clark estimated that the distance from Camp Dubois to the Mandan villages was 1,500 miles. He was only off by 100 miles. This estimate was not simply the product of good guesswork. Both he and Meriwether Lewis had done their homework and were extremely well prepared for the first leg of the trip. Clark estimated the second—and more important—leg of the journey would be 1,550 miles. In this estimate, he was off by 1,000 miles! In a testament to the captains' planning and extraordinary leadership skills, however, the Corps of Discovery was still able to survive. Their superior planning ensured that they didn't run out of the essentials; their other traits made certain that what they had not prepared for, they could compensate for through meticulous attention to detail and efficiency.

Scores of seemingly insignificant decisions and actions throughout the twenty-eight-month expedition, when viewed separately, almost do not warrant mention. But when viewed in total, they create a compelling picture of Lewis and Clark's marvelous leadership skills. A perfect example of this occurred in the days before the Corps of Discovery caught up with the Shoshone Indians, upon whom they were relying for horses. At the time, the captains were nervous that they would either scare the Shoshone away or, alternatively, invite attack before they could communicate their peaceful intentions. William Clark, therefore, before he allowed his men to go hunting with their guns, ordered the team (himself included) to walk four miles ahead and then reverse course and walk back another three miles just to ensure there were no signs of Shoshone.

Imagine walking another seven miles at the end of a long day—a day in which no signs of Shoshone Indians had been found—just to make sure that no Indian *might* hear a gun! It was these little things that made a big difference to the Corps of Discovery's success.

There is an old adage often attributed to George Herbert, a seventeenth-century poet, which goes like this:

> For want of a nail, the shoe is lost
> For want of a shoe, the horse is lost
> For want of the horse, the rider is lost
> For want of the rider, the battle is lost
> For want of a battle, the war is lost

For want of the war, the nation is lost
All for the want of a horseshoe nail

There were hundreds of potential "nails" that Lewis and Clark could have overlooked. To their immense credit, they didn't overlook any "nails" that were essential to keeping the enterprise together. The reason is because they thought long and hard about what might lie around the next bend in the river or what was just over the horizon. In fact, they never stopped thinking about the future.

CHAPTER FOUR

HONORING DIFFERENCES
The Principle of Diversity

There is very little difference between one man and another; but what little there is, is very important. This distinction seems to me to go to the root of the matter.
  —William James, in "The Will to Believe"

Meriwether Lewis's instructions to William Clark prior to the expedition's getting under way were very clear: "Find and engage some good hunters, stout, healthy, unmarried men, accustomed to the woods, and capable of bearing bodily fatigue in a pretty considerable degree." In short, they weren't just looking for any warm body. They had to measure up to some pretty high physical standards. Alexander Willard, one of the few who successfully measured up, estimated that the captains weaned out over a hundred men on physical qualifications alone. Physical strength and stamina, however, were not enough. Intelligence and discipline were also highly valued.

"A Judicious Scelection of Our Men"

To the captains' credit, they did not engage the services of a single person on the basis of social status. As Clark wrote in a letter, "Several young men have applied to accompany us—as they are not accustomed to labour and as that is a verry assential part of the Services required of the party, I am causious in giving them any encouragement." Lewis responded back to his friend that he was most pleased with his decision and reminded Clark that the selection of men was their most important job. The expedition, he said, "must depend on a judicious scelection of our men; their qualifications should be such as fit them for service; outherwise they will reather clog than further the objects in view . . . they will not answer our purpose." In other words, merit was to be the sole criterion.

In their search for talent, the captains cast the widest possible net for applicants. Invitations were sent to military forts in Ohio, Kentucky, Tennessee, and Mississippi, and notices were posted throughout the western frontier soliciting volunteers. Lewis even sought and received the support of his superior in Washington, Secretary of War Henry Dearborn, for the ability to select any person of his choosing from the ranks of other officers in the region. In fact, Dearborn sent word to the commanders of the various military forts in the west that "if any [man] in your company should be disposed to join Capt. Lewis you *will* detach them accordingly."

One of the men they added to their expedition with this newfound authority was Patrick Gass, whose military commander did not want to release him because of his unique skills as a carpenter. Gass was a grizzled veteran who had already traveled down the

Mississippi River, gone to Cuba, and then come back to the United States and traveled down the Ohio River.[1] While all the reasons for his selection are not known, Gass held true to the overall description of men being "stout" and "accustomed to the woods," and his selection appears to demonstrate the captains had a clear preference for men with unique skills. In Gass's case, he was a master carpenter, a trade that was vital for fort making and canoe building.

John Shields, about whom Lewis once wrote, "The party owes much to the injinuity of this man," was a very competent black-smith, a skill both captains knew was essential to success on the frontier. In fact, it was so valuable that the captains willingly vio-lated their own selection criteria to get Shields. He was one of only two married men allowed to go on the expedition.

A number of other individuals also brought unique skills to the expedition. Private Joseph Whitehouse was a tailor, Silas Goodrich was a talented fisherman, and John Colter and the Field brothers were excellent hunters. When the captains could not find the nec-essary talent within the existing ranks of the U.S Army, they recruited from the outside, as they did with Pierre Cruzatte, the master boatman who deftly guided the Corps of Discovery's keel-boat up the Missouri River past sandbars and floating trees, and Francis Labiche, whose skills as a tracker and interpreter proved extremely useful. And when even recruitment was not possible, the captains did what was necessary and paid the going wage to employ the best. In their case, the best was George Droulliard. He was one of the few civilians (with the exception of Clark's slave York, who could not serve in the Army because of his race, Charbonneau, and Sacagawea) to accompany the trip. Droulliard has been called "one of the two or three most valuable men on the expedition," and others have referred to him as the "third officer."[2]

Droulliard was the expedition's best hunter and a skilled interpreter who knew how to barter with the Indians. He could also steer a canoe, trap a beaver, round up horses, and describe areas so well that Clark felt comfortable mapping areas to which Droulliard had personally traveled.

What makes all of these selections so interesting is that the men were all so different. George Droulliard was half Shawnee Indian. Patrick Gass was just one generation removed from Ireland, and another member of the party, John Potts, had been born in Germany. John Shields and John Colter were raised, respectively, in Virginia and Kentucky. John Ordway was from New Hampshire and Silas Goodrich from Massachusetts. Pierre Cruzatte and Francis Labiche were half Omaha Indian and half French. Add in Toussaint Charbonneau, who was a French-Canadian Catholic; York, the black slave; and Sacagawea, the Shoshone Indian, and you have a team that would rival today's most diverse work environment. This eclectic and diverse group of individuals is a physical manifestation of Lewis and Clark's fourth leadership principle, honoring differences: the principle of diversity.

It didn't have to be this way. The captains were free to select whomever they wanted. To their credit, they did not just select people who were like them socially or culturally or from the same geographical area. They selected people regardless of their background. In fact, only George Shannon, the youngest member of the expedition, could be said to have come from a background comparable to Lewis and Clark's own upbringing. But even this selection is intriguing because Shannon was clearly chosen on the basis of talent. At the beginning of the expedition, he was eighteen years old—and because birth records were so poor at the time, he may have been as young as sixteen. The captains clearly saw something special in Shannon that they did not see in the other "young men" who wanted to join the expedition but were turned away because they lacked the "right stuff."

The end result was that Lewis and Clark, by garnering applicants from different geographic areas, various cultures, and a range of ages, virtually guaranteed a cross section of skills that would be useful to the expedition. For example, being from New Hampshire, John Ordway would have been accustomed to the colder conditions. Those members from the Appalachian or Blue Ridge regions may have possessed unique mountaineering skills, while those who grew up near the Ohio and Mississippi rivers would have been more likely to be skilled in river navigation.

The mixture of cultures—Irish, German, French, English, as well as the various Indian tribes—also ensured that different perspectives and approaches were applied to the same problem. From cooking food and trapping beaver to repairing equipment and communicating with Indians, the wealth of different perspectives and approaches inherently increased the odds of success by ensuring that the most effective method for a given problem would be employed.

Learning the Value of Diversity

It is perhaps one of history's more poignant ironies that the two most famous members of the expedition (after Lewis and Clark themselves) were Sacagawea and York. They are unique not because they were the two most important members (although you will see they were both incredibly valuable), but rather because both were in their positions involuntarily. York was the slave of William Clark, and Sacagawea was the wife of Toussaint Charbonneau and was, for all practical purposes, a slave as well.

The captains, by virtue of their upbringing, were not possessed of any experience prior to the expedition that would have led them to believe either Sacagawea or York could add much value to the expedition beyond the laborious performance of daily chores. Yet, early in the journey, it was clear that Lewis and Clark, as well as the other members of the party, had come to appreciate the value of these two distinct members.

Sacagawea: "Equal in Fortitude and Resolution"

The familiar historical picture of Sacagawea acting as Lewis and Clark's guide to the Pacific is a myth. This is unfortunate not only because it ascribes historical untruths to Sacagawea, but because it detracts from those aspects of her service that were truly important to the Corps of Discovery's success.

Sacagawea's value to the expedition was almost immediate. Even as a sixteen-year-old teenager, Sacagawea was, by virtue of her culture and her sex, already skilled in—and knowledgeable of—the realities of life on the western plains. She knew how to construct shelters, make and repair clothing, and, most important, find and preserve food. It was in this latter capacity that she first distinguished herself by finding wild licorice and artichokes for her fellow expedition members. Later in the journey, she added wild onions and fennel roots to the men's diets. While this might sound insignificant, to a group of men subsisting almost solely on meat, the inclusion of vegetables added a much needed nutritional element to their diets. Moreover, her knowledge of which plants were poisonous and which were edible helped keep the Corps of Discovery healthy.

Less than a month after joining the expedition at the Mandan villages, Sacagawea demonstrated her value as a working member of the party when a sudden gust of wind nearly capsized the main pirogue—and, along with it, valuable equipment and supplies, including the journals. With her husband temporarily paralyzed by fear (Charbonneau only stayed with the boat because Pierre Cruzatte threatened to shoot him if he didn't), Sacagawea, with a baby on her back and water pouring over the side, coolly maintained her composure and saved a number of articles that otherwise would have been lost. Her grace under pressure caused Lewis to write that her actions were "equal [in] fortitude and resolution" to any person onboard.

Not less than two weeks later, Sacagawea demonstrated a new skill to the party when she examined a pair of moccasins that the captains found and determined, by virtue of their design, the tribe to which they belonged. In this manner, she confirmed her worth as a gatherer of intelligence. Still later in the expedition, Sacagawea explained to the captains that bark missing from a tree was a sign that Indians had recently been in the area. Such information may, on the surface, appear to be of minimal use, but to Lewis and Clark, who had to base a number of decisions (e.g., camp location, size of hunting parties, and so on) on the perceived threat, such information was extremely beneficial. For instance, if hostile Indians were believed to be in the area, the captains would take extraordinary steps to conceal their presence and post extra guards. Sacagawea's knowledge was thus instrumental to the Corps of Discovery's safety at various times.

One of the next indications that Meriwether Lewis was beginning to recognize Sacagawea's worth occurred in June 1805, as she lay very ill. In his journal entry, Lewis, who was tending to her illness, noted that the expedition depended on her because she was "our only dependence for a friendly negociation with the Snake [Shoshone] Indians on whom we depend for horses to assist us in our portage from the Missouri to the Columbia River."

As the summer dragged on and the expedition had yet to find the Shoshone, it was Sacagawea who gave them hope that they were on the right track. In early August 1805, when things were starting to look desperate, Lewis noted that "the Indian woman recognized the point of a high plain...which she informed us was not very distant from the summer retreat of her nation." This time her information bolstered the spirits of the members and gave the co-commanders enough confidence to dispatch a small team to find the Shoshone.

At this point it is interesting to note that Lewis did not bring Sacagawea on his trip to find the Shoshone. It was a somewhat surprising decision, given that he did not know the language and Sacagawea would have been able to instantly communicate the expedition's peaceful intentions. One plausible explanation is that Lewis feared the team might first encounter the hostile Blackfeet Indians, and he did not want to unnecessarily endanger Sacagawea and her baby (whom she was still nursing). The more likely explanation, however, is that Lewis had an overinflated estimation of his own skills as a negotiator.

Because Lewis was ultimately successful, it is impossible to fault his decision, but Sacagawea continued to play an important role with the Shoshone. After Lewis finally located the tribe, he still had to convince them to follow him back upriver to meet up with the rest of his party. It substantially helped his cause to be able to explain that a woman of their nation was accompanying his party. And in one of history's luckiest coincidences, Sacagawea, who had been kidnapped by the Hidatsa Indians when she was only eleven years old, was reunited with her brother Cameahwait, the chief of the Shoshone. The incident undoubtedly secured the Corps of Discovery's peaceful relations with the Shoshone.

Even after this incident, Sacagawea still had more to offer. Apparently, her relationship with her brother was not enough to convince the Shoshone to postpone their annual trip to the east to hunt for buffalo, and they were intending to secretly abandon the expedition well before they had helped the party complete their arduous portage. Sacagawea, who understood the Shoshone language, overheard members of her tribe talking about their plan. She immediately relayed this information to her husband, who inexplicably kept the news to himself for a few hours before telling Captain Lewis. Upon hearing the plot, Lewis was "much mortified" and instantly sought clarification from Cameahwait. Told that it was true, Lewis was able to shame the chief into maintaining his word.

The story is extremely important because Sacagawea could have simply kept quiet—out of loyalty to her people. Instead, she demonstrated that her loyalty was to the Corps of Discovery. Had it not been, the entire expedition might have very well suffered a fatal blow. After all, the Corps of Discovery was still many miles from their destination and had a great deal of equipment and supplies to transport. Without horses and the additional manpower (and woman power) that the Shoshone provided, it would have been virtually impossible for the expedition to succeed on its own.

As with most myths, there is actually an element of truth to Sacagawea acting as a guide to the Corps of Discovery, although the lone recorded instance occurred on their return trip, well after they had already reached the Pacific and Clark had split off from Lewis to explore the Yellowstone River. Still, in July 1806, Clark thought enough of Sacagawea to write in his journal that she had "been of great service to me as a pilot through this . . . country."

Finally, it is difficult to assess how Sacagawea's mere presence influenced the men of the expedition. As the only woman in the party and as a nursing mother (recall she single-handedly carried her infant on her back for 5,000 miles), she may well have added an element of humanity to the journey and provided some added motivation for the men to return to their own loved ones. It is telling, I believe, that Clark became so fond of Sacagawea and her baby that after the expedition was over, he adopted the baby and raised him as his own son.

What is beyond question, however, is that Sacagawea served as a physical symbol of the Corps of Discovery's peaceful intentions. The Shoshone, as well as other Indian tribes Lewis and Clark encountered, were of the opinion that no warring party would willingly bring along a woman and infant. In fact, the Nez Percé Indians, whom Lewis and Clark met on the western side of the Rockies, were only convinced of the expedition's peaceful intentions *after* they saw Sacagawea.

York: "Big Medicine"

In the eighteenth century, in most states, it was illegal for a slave to be instructed in how to operate a gun. In fact, it was a punishable offense if a slave was caught carrying a gun. York, William Clark's black slave, not only knew how to operate a gun (which at the time was not like today's easy load-and-fire variety), but was permitted to carry one throughout the expedition. Moreover, he was even allowed to hunt on his own.

These facts are important because it is clear from the captains' journals that York was not just Clark's slave, he was a fully functioning, fully trusted member of the expedition.

Early in the expedition, the journals note that York swam to a "sandbar to geather Greens for our dinner." The story is worthy because it demonstrates that York could swim—something that could not be said of a number of the members of the expedition (this fact is a little surprising, given that the bulk of the trip was to take place on a river). York's swimming abilities ensured that on all of the dangerous rafting trips, when many of the other party members were left on the shore to walk the route, he shouldered more than his share of responsibility for the safe execution of the raft.

York's value was not limited to hunting and rafting trips. By the journals' account, whenever Clark went out on a particularly harrowing mission, York was consistently at his side, sharing fully in the trip's fatigues and dangers. This suggests that Clark was extremely confident of York's skills and his ability to handle himself in the event of an emergency or an Indian attack. That Clark trusted York, late in the journey, to trade with the Indians suggests that he thought of York as being of equal intelligence to the other members of the expedition.

Neither was York's value limited to his tangible skills. By virtue of his skin color, he was a great mystery to the Indians. They referred to him as "Big Medicine," a term used by the Indians for phenomena that they couldn't explain. Far from considering him a lesser individual because of his skin color, the Indians perceived York as being of greater value. Some, in fact, perceived his blackness as a sign of courage. According to Robert Betts, the author of *In Search of York*, the Indians were "awed by York's singularity." This "singularity" served as more than just an interesting antidote to the rest of the men in the expedition. Betts speculates that "York's blackness served the expedition as a passport to western tribes who were so curious . . . they greeted the white visitors more cordially than they might have otherwise done." In one instance, when the Shoshone were thinking of leaving the expedition, Betts suggests that word of York's presence may have been the "decisive factor—in making it possible for them to obtain horses and continue on."

In a final testament to York's value, it is worth noting that William Clark ultimately freed York a few years after the expedition returned to St. Louis (although the delay is believed to have been the cause of a serious rift between Clark and York).[3]

Leading Into the Unknown

Most of today's corporations, by design or necessity, are extending into new markets and new geographies—a situation that is not noticeably different from that of Lewis and Clark. Once the captains decided to lead the expedition, they had no choice but to move into unknown territories. To a great extent, they didn't know whom or what they were going to encounter, but by selecting people with a variety of skills and hailing from a multitude of cultures, they were reasonably well prepared to handle many different situations. Among the tangible lessons that today's business executive can learn from Lewis and Clark's approach to diversity are the following:

Diversity's value must be cultivated. By necessity, Lewis and Clark were required to utilize Sacagawea and York in capacities that they would likely never have been given the opportunity to fill in normal society. What the captains came to understand is that when given the chance, Sacagawea and York performed equal to anyone else in the expedition. In many cases, they had skills that the captains were probably not even aware of. The lesson for business leaders is that diversity, like many assets, must be actively cultivated. One company that is taking a proactive approach to cultivating diversity is Shell Oil Company. Eager to capture the greater creativity and innovative problem-solving skills that diversity has been shown to create, Shell not only benchmarks itself against the diversity levels of other global leaders, but makes a point of asking its employees, on an annual basis, how the company can better utilize and develop people's skills.

Diversity has intangible value. The very fact that York and Sacagawea were physically different contributed to the Corps of Discovery's success. Sacagawea, by virtue of her womanhood, brought an element of humanity to the expedition and helped convince Indian tribes of the expedition's peaceful intentions; and York's blackness was so intriguing to the Indians that they were more open to the Corps of Discovery. This point is important because some businesses may feel that people can only add value through their specific work-related experiences or qualifications. This is not necessarily true. IBM Corp. is one company that seems to understand this point. Nearly three out of five of its board of directors are women, multicultural, and/or non-U.S. born, as are nearly 40 percent of the members of IBM's Worldwide Executive Council. The same holds for people with disabilities. In addition to being just as skilled as their counterparts, disabled people may actually bring a unique perspective, based on their experience, to a particular problem.

Diversity is not just racial or ethnic. It would be easy to focus exclusively on the value that Sacagawea and York added to the Corps of Discovery, but to do so would miss out on the richness of skills, experiences, and perspectives that many other members contributed to the Corps of Discovery's success. The lesson for today's corporations is that while racial and ethnic diversity is important, diversity of sex, age, physical ability, and geography is equally important.

Forgo the familiar and hire only the best. Under no circumstances were Lewis and Clark going to select expedition members on the basis of social standing. In fact, it is clear that they went out of their way to avoid such people. Lewis and Clark hired on the basis of merit. This sentiment is captured in *The Book of Leadership Wisdom,* in which Harold S. Geneen, the former CEO of ITT Corp., wrote of his company's hiring process: "We set out to hire only the very best people . . . I did not want glamorous, glib-talking men who got by on their coiffured good looks or family connections." One of the immediate benefits of forgoing the familiar is that companies naturally must expand the pool from which they are looking for people.

A few years ago, I had the opportunity to share a speaking stage with Kevin Barth, president of the Commerce Bank in Kansas City. He related to a group of college students that one of the primary reasons he was able to rise to his current position was because early in his career, a courageous senior official at the bank recommended that they make an exception to hiring only graduates of Ivy League schools. Barth, a graduate from Graceland University, a small liberal arts college in Lamoni, Iowa, was thus hired. Today, the bank's hiring is strictly merit-based.

Cast a wide net. By soliciting members from every corner of the United States, the captains guaranteed that they were able to select from a pool of individuals who possessed a variety of different skill sets. Furthermore, the regional differences also provided a wider menu of problem-solving approaches. In an era of limited education and poor communication, the notion of adopting "best practices" wasn't a familiar concept to Lewis and Clark, but when presented with a unique problem, the captains—because their team had such different experiences—could bring a variety of approaches to bear on each issue. As a result, Lewis and Clark could either select the best method or adopt an improved hybrid approach.

Unisys Corp. is an example of a company that has specifically cast a wider net. As company policy, managers are active in a variety of special-interest professional associations in order to maximize the chances that they will come in contact with high-potential individuals of different backgrounds and cultures. They recognize that it is not enough to just pay lip service to diversity—they actively work to expose themselves to diversity.

Proceed On!

It would be unrealistic to say that Lewis and Clark started their selection process with diversity as an end goal or even a deciding factor. As products of the late-eighteenth century, this was not how they thought. The lesson, however, is that by focusing on their end goal—reaching the Pacific—they were led, by necessity, to assemble a diverse team. As the famous architect Ludwig Mies van der Rohe said, "Form follows function." And to conquer the unknown, that "form" manifested itself as a diverse team.

In the spring of 1806, as the Corps of Discovery were working their way back over the Rocky Mountains, they encountered the Walla Walla Indians. As always, the captains were interested in learning about the Indians' customs as well as any information the Walla Wallas might be able to share about the path ahead. The process of collecting this information, however, was easier said than done. In this particular case, a female Shoshone Indian who was a captive of the Walla Wallas translated the Indians' phrase into Shoshone for Sacagawea, who then translated it into Hidatsa for her French-Canadian husband, Toussaint Charbonneau. He, in turn, translated it into French for Francis Labiche, a private in the

Corps of Discovery who was half French and half Omaha Indian, who then had the responsibility of converting it into English for the captains. Phrase by phrase, back and forth, sometimes for the better part of a day, Lewis and Clark queried the locals.

I recount this story not because it was a unique event—similar translations were repeated throughout the expedition and various members of the expedition were called into service at various times—but rather because it serves as a wonderful reminder that success is dependent on the unique talents of every member of the team.

A more recent example of the benefit of diversity was demonstrated by Ford Motor Company a few years ago when it formed a team to redesign the Ford Windstar minivan. By including women, mothers, and older and disabled drivers, the team came up with a number of new improvements and innovations, including a "sleeping baby" mode for overhead lights, easy-to-reach cup holders to prevent spills, and a reverse-sensing accident avoidance system to signal an alarm when objects are in the way. These seemingly minor—almost invisible—improvements had a significant effect on sales because they added real value to a larger pool of potential customers by addressing real-world concerns.

The point of these two stories is that diversity, far from just being a "feel good," politically correct policy, offers a real competitive advantage to companies that make the effort. It is a lesson Lewis and Clark learned over the course of their long, arduous journey, and it is a lesson business leaders should take to heart if they want to remain competitive in the future.

CHAPTER FIVE

EQUITABLE JUSTICE
The Principle of Compassionate Discipline

*The unfailing formula for the production of
morale is . . . discipline . . . joined with fair
treatment. . . .*

—General Douglas MacArthur

James Ronda, Lewis and Clark scholar and author of *Lewis and Clark Among the Indians*, has referred to the members of the expedition as "a wild bunch of hard drinking, brawling, and insubordinate rowdies."[1] Almost to a man, they were young, energetic, and experienced frontiersmen who had survived because of their ability to handle themselves as individuals. They were not men to whom the concept of "team" was a natural fit. By all accounts, the first few months at Camp Dubois, as they waited to depart on the expedition, were not easy ones. The men were still feeling each other out, as well as feeling out their commanders.

Furthermore, the cold winter weather and lack of physical activity easily led to boredom and restlessness, and their proximity to civilization made whiskey easy to obtain. The combination of factors led to a lot of early trouble.

In early 1804, Lewis had to visit St. Louis to purchase supplies and Clark was away on similar business. The captains verbally issued orders that in their absence, Sergeant John Ordway was to be in command. When they returned, they were shocked to learn that two men had refused to stand guard duty—saying they were only going to take orders from the captains. Another three soldiers went into town and got drunk.

Lewis and Clark immediately reestablished order. The entire team was called out and the men were told, in no uncertain terms, that when they were away, Sergeant Ordway was in command. The captains then drafted written orders stating that "the ultimate success of the enterprise in which we all embarked" required absolute allegiance to the chain of command. Lewis noted that he thought John Shields and Reuben Field, the two members guilty of insubordination to Ordway, were better soldiers than they had demonstrated, so the captains let them off with only a verbal reprimand. Lewis and Clark's confidence in the two was repeatedly repaid throughout the course of the expedition, as neither man was again guilty of any significant infraction. The three members who got drunk were ordered confined to camp for ten days.

A few weeks later, when both captains were again away, some of the men got drunk and took to fighting. Upon his return to camp, Captain Clark administered justice swiftly. He ordered some of the men to build a cabin for a local woman, and the others were assigned various chores, such as packing and repacking the keelboat. The punishments were not overly harsh and thus did not undermine morale, but served as enough of a deterrent to defend against repeat incidents. A side benefit was that the men's time was put to constructive use.

Lewis and Clark's approach to punishment, however, changed noticeably immediately upon disembarking from Camp Dubois. Three days into the journey, on May 17, 1804, Private John Collins was court-martialed for being AWOL and showing disrespect to his commanding officer. He was promptly found guilty and sentenced to receive fifty lashes. Privates William Werner and Hugh Hall were similarly found guilty of being AWOL and received twenty-five lashes.

The punishments clearly set a tone for the remainder of the expedition and informed the members that the price for disobeying the rules would be swift and harsh. The captains' approach was a sharp contrast to their preexpedition discipline, which was limited to confinement and extra chores. The reason for the change was that the expedition was now officially under way and they were on a military mission of great national importance. Furthermore, the captains understood that adherence to the rules might literally mean the difference between life and death, and therefore punishment would be administered as necessary to keep order.

The captains' differing approach to discipline lies at the heart of their fifth leadership principle, equitable justice: the principle of compassionate discipline.

Discipline: A Means to an End

A month later, in late June of 1804, Private Collins was court-martialed for "getting drunk on his post" and his cohort, Private Hall, was court-martialed for drawing whiskey out of the barrel without authorization. Collins received a hundred lashes and Hall received fifty. What is interesting is that in this instance, neither Lewis nor Clark presided over the court-martial. They instead allowed Collins and Hall's peers to decide on the punishment. The incident is significant because it illustrates how the captains used discipline for purposes other than establishing order. In this case, the decision highlighted for everyone that Collins and Hall's crime was not so much a direct threat to Lewis and Clark's authority as it was a violation of the trust of their peers from whom they were stealing. It therefore helped reinforce the notion that they were a team and may help explain why the incident was the only such violation on the expedition.

The decision is also intriguing because it stands in marked contrast to their first court-martial of Collins and the subsequent court-martial of Alexander Willard, who, two weeks later, was court-martialed for falling asleep on guard duty. In both instances, Lewis and Clark constituted the court-martial and decided the penalty. In Willard's case, they did not believe his plea, which was that he was guilty of *lying down* but not guilty of *sleeping*, and ordered a hundred lashes.

The punishment may appear overly harsh, but the fact that this was the only instance of someone falling asleep on duty is important to note because almost ten months later—and exactly one year from the date of the first court-martial—the sergeant of the guard woke up the captains and alerted them to a burning tree that moments later came crashing down in the exact spot where they had been lying. In Lewis's words, they would have been "crushed to atoms" had they not been warned. Two weeks later, a sentinel helped steer a stampeding buffalo away from some men who were sleeping. I recount these facts because it is entirely possible that Lewis and Clark's early administration of discipline reminded everyone of what was at stake and helped ensure no one ever again fell asleep on guard duty. Discipline was thus used as a means to prevent future mistakes—and tragedies.

In August 1804, Lewis and Clark faced perhaps their most serious challenge when Moses Reed deserted the party and took a rifle with him. The captains immediately ordered their best man, George Droulliard, to go out and find him. They gave him instructions to shoot Reed, if necessary. The order was not necessary because Reed was peacefully returned to camp and summarily court-martialed. Reed pleaded for leniency and Clark noted that he would be as favorable as his oath of office allowed. Reed's act was a serious threat to the operational strength of the expedition, and thus he was shown no mercy. He was given a hundred lashes, the most permitted under the Army's Articles of War, and was "not to be considered in the future as one of the Party." The punishment sent a strong message that no person was so important that he was above being removed. In many ways, this portion of the penalty was more "painful" than the physical lashes because it meant Reed would not receive the extra pay, the land warrants, and, perhaps most important, the prestige and honor of being called a member of the permanent party of the Corps of Discovery. (Reed was kept on until April 1805, when he was sent back with the return party.)

The next disciplinary incident occurred as the expedition approached Fort Mandan in October 1804. A court-martial was convened for John Newman for "having uttered repeated expressions of a highly criminal and mutinous nature." Lewis and Clark went on to note that his acts had the tendency of not only destroying "every principle of military discipline, but also to alienate the affections of individuals composing this Detachment to their officers, and disaffect them to the service for which they have been so sacredly and solemnly engaged."

This incident is revealing for a number of reasons. First, the term *repeated expressions* implies that Newman's mutinous comments were not a one-time affair but rather reflected a pattern the captains could not allow to go unchallenged. A lone comment, uttered in the heat of an argument, it appears may have been forgiven, but not repeated utterances. Second, in this case, Lewis and Clark again gave the power of determining the punishment over to the enlisted men. The journals note that Clark presided over the court-martial but would only "attend to the forms & rules of a president without giving his opinion." Neither man elaborated on his rationale, but it demonstrated a remarkable amount of trust in the enlisted men and helped the remaining members come together as a team.

History will never know what would have happened had the men found Newman not guilty or had Lewis and Clark otherwise disagreed with the penalty because Newman's peers unanimously found him guilty and ordered him to be punished with seventy-five lashes on his bare back. The sentence was approved and Newman was disbanded from the party. Although none of the enlisted men ever commented on the punishment in their journals, their decision suggests that they understood that a direct challenge to the captains' authority threatened the military cohesiveness of the expedition, and this, in turn, undermined the odds of their success.

Flexibility

What is interesting about Lewis and Clark's approach to discipline is how flexible it was. While they never shied away from administering discipline, they applied it in different measures and by different methods according to the crime. In the beginning, when it was Sergeant Ordway's authority being questioned and not their own, the captains—recognizing the need for military order but sensing that the unit was still learning about each other as well as their boundaries—simply issued written orders explaining the rules and confined to camp some of the men who had disobeyed Ordway. When the soldiers fought among themselves, Clark ordered them to engage in constructive tasks as a way of disciplining the men. In many ways, this was an effective approach because many of the early troublemakers never again displayed any problems.

However, once the expedition got under way, the whip came out and the tone was set very quickly. But even in these matters, the captains demonstrated flexibility. When two of the men were caught stealing whiskey, Lewis and Clark turned to the men's peers to administer justice. However, when Willard was found guilty of sleeping on duty, the captains convened the court-martial themselves and prescribed the punishment. If a particular crime seriously jeopardized the safety of the entire expedition, Lewis and Clark were not about to delegate the responsibility for administering justice.

The difference in handling Reed's desertion and Newman's mutinous acts is also instructive. Reed's act jeopardized the entire party by reducing their fighting power. In Newman's case, the act was less an immediate threat to the expedition and more of a challenge to the captains' direct authority. By allowing the enlisted men to make the decision—and by trusting them to make a proper decision—Lewis and Clark actually enhanced their own standing because the verdict suggested that the other members of the expedition understood that the success of the mission rested in large part on the other members adhering to the captains' authority.

The final court-martial occurred on February 9, 1805, when Private Thomas Howard returned to the fort after the main gate had been closed for the night and scaled the wall. In so doing, Howard exposed the vulnerability of the fort, which was demonstrated when a local Indian followed Howard's example and climbed over the wall, entering the fort without permission. The details of the court-martial are not provided, but Lewis and Clark noted that they administered a harsher penalty than usual—fifty lashes—because Howard was a more experienced soldier and they felt he should have shown better judgment.

In many ways, it is a fitting final punishment because it demonstrates the three cornerstones of the captains' approach to discipline. It demonstrated flexibility because it took into consideration Howard's seniority; it served a higher end by reminding the other men that there were still potential dangers; and it demonstrated that no one was above the enforcement of discipline.

"Most Perfect Harmony"

In the spring of 1805, the Corps of Discovery departed their winter headquarters and ventured into territory that had never been explored by any American. As Meriwether Lewis recorded, "We were now about to penetrate a country at least two thousand miles in width, on which the foot of civilized man had never trodden; the good or evil it had in store for us was for experiment yet to determine." He then added, "[T]he party are in excellent health and sperits, zealously attached to the enterprise, and anxious to proceed; not a whisper of murmur or discontent to be heard among, but all act in unison, and the most perfect harmony." This latter phrase, "most perfect harmony," expressed the fact that the men of the expedition now knew exactly what was expected of them.

Captain Clark—Buffalow Gangue
John Ford Clymer, oil on canvas, 1976.

The Lewis Crossing
John Ford Clymer, oil on canvas, 1973.

Courtesy of Mrs. John F. Clymer and the Clymer Museum of Art.

Salt Makers
John Ford Clymer, oil on canvas, 1975.

Courtesy of Mrs. John F. Clymer and the Clymer Museum of Art.

Sacagawea at the Big Water
John Ford Clymer, oil on canvas, 1974.

Courtesy of Mrs. John F. Clymer and the Clymer Museum of Art.

Lewis and Clark in the Bitterroots
John Ford Clymer, oil on canvas, 1967.

Lewis and Clark Meeting the Indians at Ross' Hole
Charles M. Russell, oil on canvas, 1912.

York

Charles M. Russell, watercolor, 1908.

Courtesy of the Montana Historical Society. Gift of the artist.

Up the Jefferson
John Ford Clymer, oil on canvas, 1973.

Courtesy of Mrs. John F. Clymer and the Clymer Museum of Art.

Great Falls
(at present site of Ryan Dam)

Victor Bjornberg/Travel Montana

Decision Point
(junction of Missouri and Marias Rivers, near Loma, Montana)

Donnie Sexton/Travel Montana

Hasty Retreat
John Ford Clymer, oil on canvas, circa 1970.

Courtesy of Mrs. John F. Clymer and the Clymer Museum of Art.

Meriwether Lewis
Charles Willson Peale, from life, 1807.

Courtesy of Independence National Historical Park.

William Clark
Charles Willson Peale, from life, 1807–1808.

Courtesy of Independence National Historical Park.

Equally important, the few troublemakers, specifically Moses Reed and John Newman, had been removed from the permanent party and sent back downriver.

It was at this point in the expedition that Lewis and Clark, to paraphrase Stephen Ambrose, appear to have thrown out the official rule book. From this point forward, there would be no more court-martials and no more lashings. The closest either Lewis or Clark would come was verbally "upbraiding" some members of the party. Whether it was a conscious decision on behalf of the co-commanders to forgo physical punishment is not known, but it does suggest that Lewis and Clark were aware that the expedition had now entered a new phase of the journey and that they would have to adjust their leadership style accordingly.

Almost immediately, both Lewis and Clark begin to show a deeper compassion for all of the expedition's members. In late spring, for almost two weeks, the captains tenderly cared for Sacagawea's baby, "Pomp." They even stayed up late at night to tend to his needs. A few weeks later, in June 1805, Lewis's lengthy description of Sacagawea's illness demonstrated real compassion. Eldon Chuinard, the author of *Only One Man Died*, in fact praised Lewis's handling of Sacagawea and stated that his care "would not be exceeded by any physician of [Lewis's] time."

Lewis and Clark also began to bestow more rewards on their men. The most appreciated and tangible reward was whiskey. Although their stock was getting dangerously low at this point in the journey, Lewis and Clark issued an extra gill (the equivalent of four ounces) when they reached the confluence of the Yellowstone and Missouri rivers—a noticeable accomplishment. Two weeks later, after a harrowing run-in with a grizzly bear that required ten bullets to kill, the captains calmed everyone's nerves with another gill. On June 3, when everyone in the party, with the exception of Lewis and Clark, was convinced that the north fork in the river was the true Missouri River, the captains again opened up the bottle. They did the same after the men were bloodied in a hailstorm in late June and, finally, they used up the last of their whiskey rations on July 4, in celebration of the nation's twenty-ninth birthday.

Perhaps more telling than the issuing of gills and drams of whiskey is Lewis and Clark's decision to begin rewarding members of the expedition by naming prominent physical locations in their honor. Unfortunately, because of the time delay between when Lewis and Clark first named these features and the publication of their journals many years later, most of the original names do not appear on today's maps. Regardless, the members of the party were cognizant at the time that the captains were recognizing them for their service. Rivers were named after Droulliard (although they spelled his name Drewyer), Cruzatte, Labiche, Pryor, Hall, and, most notably, Sacagawea, shortly after her courageous conduct in saving various items when the pirogue almost capsized. A number of the other men also had physical features, such as creek valleys and gulches, named after them.

Lewis and Clark did not exclusively name such features after the expedition members. President Thomas Jefferson, Secretary of War Henry Dearborn, and Secretary of the Treasury Albert Gallatin all had rivers named in their honor, as did the captains themselves. Clark even named a river after his wife-to-be, Julia Hancock, while Lewis honored his cousin, Maria Wood, by naming the Marias River after her (one of the few names that remain today). I relate these facts because they serve as a reminder that the captains were under no obligation to name any rivers, creeks, or other features of the land after the expedition members. There were plenty of other politicians to flatter back in Washington, and both Lewis and Clark came from large and distinguished families that would have taken great pleasure in having a river named after them. Their decision not to do so and instead honor the Corps of Discovery says much about the level of respect they had for their team.

A Dangerous Letdown

The captains' "softer, gentler" management style served them extremely well throughout the remainder of the expedition, with one possible exception. After leaving Fort Mandan, military order still pervaded the Corps of Discovery's daily activities. Orders were issued, tents pitched, food gathered, guards posted, items repaired, and various other tasks assigned and tended to as requested. Yet Lewis and Clark, it appears, were reluctant to administer discipline anywhere near as stern as that which they ordered early in the journey. A revealing moment occurred on May 8, 1806, as they laid up on the western side of the Bitterroots before recrossing the mountains en route to their return to St. Louis. Given a direct order to go out and hunt food, a number of men disobeyed the captains and instead choose to lay about the camp "without our permission."

A part of the men's action can be explained by their severe disappointment, after a long five months at Fort Clatsop the previous winter, at having to bide their time for almost a month while they waited for the snows to melt before starting their trip back over the Bitterroots. The explanation does not, however, condone their behavior. Lewis and Clark's decision not to discipline the men is even more difficult to understand. The men had been given a direct order, which they blatantly disobeyed. Lewis and Clark simply noted in their journal that they "severely" chided the men. In essence, they let them off with nothing more than a verbal tongue-lashing.

The decision can perhaps be rationalized by human nature. After all, by this time the Corps of Discovery had successfully reached the Pacific and the men had proved themselves capable of meeting every challenge that they had been presented. They had portaged the Greats Falls, found the Shoshone Indians, crossed the Bitterroots, and rafted the Columbia River. They had done everything the captains had asked of them and more. Furthermore, they were functioning well as a team. To administer a strict dose of punishment might have unnecessarily dampened morale. With the return trip over the Bitterroots still to come, Lewis and Clark may have reasoned that it was okay to "let this one slide." A more sympathetic explanation may simply have been that Lewis and Clark didn't feel that anything more than a verbal warning was required to correct the men's misbehavior.

Unfortunately, this more relaxed approach to discipline ultimately manifested itself in one of the Corps of Discovery's biggest mistakes. The event occurred on July 27, 1806. At this point in the return trip, Lewis and Clark had split up for a few weeks in order to explore more territory. As Clark was exploring the Yellowstone River, Lewis had ascended the Marias River deep into Blackfeet Indian territory. The previous day, he had established contact with a small party of young Blackfeet warriors. They smoked a peace pipe and then settled into a camp for the night. What transpired next can only be attributed to an uncharacteristic lapse of military discipline. Joseph Field, who was standing post, carelessly laid his gun down. The Blackfeet warriors seized the opportunity and grabbed the gun, along with the weapons of some of the other sleeping members of the party—including Lewis—each of whom had also carelessly stored his gun in such a manner that it could easily be taken. It was only through the quickness of their actions that Lewis and his small party were able to recover their guns—but the cost was steep. The party killed two Blackfeet Indians and seriously damaged the prospect that the United States would be able to establish peaceful relations with the Blackfeet, one of the most powerful Indian nations.

The unfortunate act of violence—the only one committed against Indians by the Corps of Discovery—was entirely avoidable and started a period of violent bloodshed between the United States and the Blackfeet that lasted the better part of the next half century. (Ironically, three members of the Corps of Discovery would, after the successful completion of the journey, later die at the hands of the Blackfeet. Another, John Colter, would survive only by running more than five miles after being stripped naked and given a chance to outrun a group of Blackfeet warriors.)

It is impossible to draw a direct connection between the captains' unwillingness to discipline their men and this incident—just as it is not possible to connect their harsh disciplining of Willard for falling asleep with the alertness of the guard who saved them from a burning tree months later—but it is reasonable to conclude that the more permissive attitude created an environment more ripe for a breakdown.

Leading Into the Unknown

In spite of Lewis and Clark's use of corporal punishment—which obviously could not be emulated today—there are still valuable lessons from their experiences that are applicable to contemporary leaders.

Start out easy and inform people of the rules. During the spring of 1803, when the members of the expedition were still getting to know one another, the captains didn't immediately administer discipline in a harsh form. Instead, they called everyone to order and explained the rules. They then reinforced the rules by issuing written orders. In the case of most of the soldiers, once they understood what was expected of them, there were no more disciplinary issues.

Dick Cheney, shortly after he was appointed secretary of defense in 1989, employed a similar policy. Three days into his tenure, the chief of staff of the U.S. Air Force, General Larry Welch, was quoted as contradicting the official policy of the Pentagon on the important topic of missile deployment. It was well within Cheney's power to have the general dismissed. Instead, he quickly but quite publicly rebuked the general. In so doing, Cheney set an early tone that he was in charge and was not about to let military personnel issue a policy statement that had not been cleared. To ensure that it didn't happen again, Cheney privately communicated the rules that he expected all military officers to follow during his tenure. For the remainder of his term, those rules were abided by, with one notable exception (see the next lesson). An additional benefit of having written policies for today's business executives is that by articulating clear, objective consequences for various infractions, claims of discrimination can be prevented.

Attune disciplinary tactics to the situation. General Welch's successor, General Michael Dugan, apparently did not learn the lesson of clearing all policy statements with Secretary Cheney. Just three months into his job, as the United States military was busily preparing for the first Persian Gulf War, Dugan made a series of public statements that ran counter to official U.S. policy and seriously undermined the administration's efforts to forge a united coalition against Iraq. Cheney immediately relieved the four-star general of his command. Just as Lewis and Clark changed their tactics after they departed Camp Dubois, Cheney too made a decision that reflected new realities. In his case, the United States was preparing for war, and it was imperative that he send a strong and unequivocal signal that mistakes of the nature of Dugan's could not be tolerated. In the business world, an apt analogy may be how a company needs to enforce a more stringent form of discipline in the event of substance abuse for different jobs. In some instances, there is simply a need for a "zero tolerance" policy.

Look for ways to apply discipline constructively. Lewis and Clark did not administer discipline only in one form. When they felt they could send a strong message without resorting to physical means, they looked for constructive ways to apply discipline, such as when they made their men build cabins or repair the keelboat as punishment for certain violations. In the business world, most companies can employ a range of disciplinary actions, from written and oral admonishments and reprimands to suspensions, demotions, and ultimately removal. The primary purpose of discipline is to avoid a repeat of the mistake, and managers must balance the preventive aspect of discipline with the overall goals of the mission.

When possible, look to peers to administer discipline. Lewis and Clark understood that if the mission was going to succeed, it would be on the basis of their functioning as a team. As a result, if certain actions threatened the cohesiveness of the team—rather than their own direct authority—Lewis and Clark had the members themselves decide on the penalty.

An example of situation-based discipline occurred in the locker room of the Chicago Bulls in the spring of 1993. Michael Jordan had retired (for the first time) the year before, and Scottie Pippen was widely regarded as the team's new star. In their playoff matchup against the New York Knicks, the Bulls lost the first two games. With three seconds left in game three and trailing 101–100, the Bulls were on the brink of elimination in the best-of-five game series. Phil Jackson, then head coach of the Bulls, called a timeout and diagrammed the final shot. It did not have Pippen shooting the ball. Miffed at Jackson's call, Pippen sulked on the end of the bench and refused to go back on the court. Jackson ordered another player to take his place. The play was executed perfectly; Tony Kukoc sank the shot, and the Bulls won the game.

The post-game celebration was muted because of Pippen's stunning act of disobedience. Furthermore, Pippen's act had directly challenged Jackson's authority. Jackson knew he had to do something. But rather than take on Pippen directly and make it an issue between him and his star player, Jackson ordered the team to discuss the situation and resolve it themselves. Jackson knew that while Pippen's disobedience was a direct challenge to his leadership, the greater issue was that Pippen had let the team down. The result was that the team had a constructive airing of the issues and Jackson redirected his team's focus. The Bulls won the next game before falling to the Knicks in the final game.[2]

When necessary, do it yourself. There are times in business—as well as in life—when the issue of discipline simply cannot be delegated. For instance, when a leader's direct authority is undermined or an employee's action threatens the success of an organization's mission, discipline must come from the top. Lewis and Clark demonstrated this lesson when they assumed responsibility for determining Willard's punishment when he fell asleep on guard duty. They did so because they understood his action jeopardized the safety of the entire expedition.

Understand that positive incentives work better in uncertain times. After Fort Mandan, as the Corps of Discovery entered undiscovered territory, Lewis and Clark adopted a more positive, incentive-based system of motivation. This was because a premium was placed on operational flexibility. In many ways, this situation is analogous to today's business environment. Business conditions are changing so fast that employees cannot afford to be constrained with policies for every single situation. The best way to ensure success in such situations is to provide positive incentives. One reason so many companies offer perks in the form of employee recognition events and flex time is because it gives business leaders a tangible way to reward initiative and creative thinking. Businesses can, by example, demonstrate the type of behavior they are looking to cultivate in their employees.

Accept that discipline will always be necessary. Many business leaders have undoubtedly experienced a situation similar to that which Lewis and Clark faced when some of their men disobeyed a direct order. And like Lewis and Clark, they may have chosen to ignore it because they considered it a one-time event or, alternatively, a rare mistake by a good employee. It is a greater mistake, however, to let such actions slide because they can manifest themselves long afterward. For instance, if it is company policy to "always do what is in the best interest of customers," even the best employees cannot be allowed to avoid some form of discipline if they violate this cardinal rule.

Proceed On!

The long-term success of the Corps of Discovery's mission required that certain rules be adhered to and certain jobs performed. To not follow these rules or to not execute the jobs would have threatened the success of the mission. While the punishment was severe at times, the consequences of failure would have been higher. Lewis and Clark also understood, however, that there was no one-size-fits-all approach to discipline and that the unique and demanding nature of the journey required flexibility. For instance, when the Corps of Discovery was just starting to come together as a team in the winter of 1803, the captains gave the members the benefit of the doubt. Once the expedition got under way, the punishments became far more physical and served as a reminder of what was at stake. Once they entered uncharted territory, the old way of punishment went out the window. The whip was put away and never taken out again. It was as though they were literally leaving the old world view of management behind and adopting a new method. The new method was based less on discipline and military order and more on compassion and positive motivation.

And if the final result is the indicator, Lewis and Clark chose wisely. Private Joseph Whitehouse, in a letter written after the expedition, praised the "humanity shown by the captains at all times." And even Alexander Willard, the man who had received a hundred lashes for falling asleep at his post, would later name one son Lewis and another Clark. It is a fitting tribute to Lewis and Clark's leadership skills that a man who bore the permanent scars of their discipline still felt enough respect for both captains to name his own sons in their honor. It is a wonderful example for understanding how discipline, when mixed appropriately with fairness and compassion, can lead not only to success but to long-lasting respect.

ABSOLUTE RESPONSIBILITY
The Principle of Leading from the Front

And when at some future date the high court
of history sits in judgment on each of us . . .
our success or failure . . . will be measured by
the answers to four questions: Were we truly
men of courage . . . Were we truly men of
judgment . . . Were we truly men of integrity
. . . Were we truly men of dedication?
—President John F. Kennedy

On September 25, 1804, Lewis and Clark met with the Teton Sioux for the first time. The negotiations went poorly. The Americans lacked a skilled interpreter and had a difficult time communicating. The resulting confusion, combined with cultural ignorance on both sides, made misinterpretation easy. The captains' insistence on selecting one chief to represent all the others and giving him more gifts than the other chiefs did nothing to improve the situation, nor did the Teton Sioux's demands for more gifts. Lewis and Clark only added "fuel to the fire" by dispensing whiskey.

All these factors created a recipe for an explosive situation. One of the slighted chiefs, a man named the Partisan, insisted on more gifts. Three young Sioux warriors, working on the Partisan's behalf, then seized the bow cable of the boat and refused to let it go. Clark was not about to be intimidated or coerced. He was an experienced Indian fighter and on a mission to represent his government. Clark demanded that the cable be released. When his repeated requests went unheeded, he felt himself grow "warm" and drew his sword. Alerted to the ensuing crisis, Meriwether Lewis quickly ordered the keelboat's cannons to be readied. The men of the Corps of Discovery cocked their rifles and took up positions behind the boat's protective shielding.

On the shore, hundreds of Sioux warriors lined the banks. They laced their bows with arrows and drew them taut. A massive and bloody fight was just moments away. Then Black Buffalo, one of the other chiefs, ordered the warriors to release the cable. The situation was defused.

Had Black Buffalo not diplomatically resolved the situation, the journey of the Corps of Discovery might have ended right there, and the course of history would have forever been altered because the Corps of Discovery—although it possessed superior firepower in terms of rifles and cannons—would have ultimately succumbed to the Sioux's greater numbers. With a victory, the Sioux would have taken into their possession all of the Corps of Discovery's guns and ammunition, and it would have taken the United States years to recover and mount an effective counter-campaign against the now well-armed Indian nation. Among the first casualties of the conflict would have been Meriwether Lewis and William Clark.

Obviously, this scenario did not play out. The reason is that both men stood their ground—or as Stephen Ambrose wrote, they "refused to back down,"—thereby earning the grudging respect of the Teton Sioux by accepting full responsibility, with all of its potential deadly consequences, for their actions. In so doing, the captains forced the Sioux to capitulate and demonstrated the sixth leadership principle, absolute responsibility: the principle of leading from the front.

In addition to this poignant example, there were three other important situations during the expedition when Lewis and Clark placed themselves in the position of leading from the front. Those three moments were the crucial decision at the Marias River, when the captains had to determine which fork in the river represented the Missouri River; their search for the Shoshone Indians; and their historic struggle over the Bitterroot Mountains.

The Decision at the Marias

On June 2, 1805, in the fading sunlight of dusk, Lewis and Clark came "to the entrance of a very considerable river." The river split into two branches of roughly equal size, well past "The River Which Scolds at All Others" (now called the Milk River), which Lewis and Clark had been told was the last river before reaching the Great Falls. According to all the intelligence they had received the previous winter from the Hidatsa Indians and others, this new river wasn't supposed to be there. Yet there it was. In a great understatement, Lewis wrote, this fact "astonishes us a little."

Darkness fell and it was too late for the captains to examine the river that evening, so the Corps of Discovery chose to set up camp on the south side of the Missouri. Upon awaking the next morning, the party moved directly below the junction of the two rivers. "An interesting question was now to be determined," wrote Lewis in his journal, "which of these was the Missouri[?]"

It was more than an interesting, academic question. It was a question fraught with danger. The party needed to reach the Rockies and find the Shoshone Indians if they were to acquire the horses they would need to portage to the head of the Columbia River and reach the Pacific before winter closed in. "[T]o mistake the stream at this period of the season, two months of the traveling season having now elapsed . . . would not only loose us the whole of this season but would probably so dishearten the party that it might defeat the expedition altogether," Lewis wrote.

Lewis and Clark faced their most important decision to date, and for the first time since the party had left the Mandan villages, they realized the intelligence that they had been provided was wrong. In hindsight, the explanation was relatively straightforward. The Hidatsa Indians disdained the slowness of boats and preferred to travel by horseback. As a result, they cut across the land between the bends in the Missouri and therefore missed this river. In recounting for the captains what lay ahead of them, the Indians were unable to warn them of this fork in the river because they had never encountered it.[1]

This story represents a rare mistake on the part of the captains. Even if they could not have learned about the fork in the river, had they been more thorough in their inquiries the previous winter, they might have anticipated some surprises by virtue of the fact that the method by which the Hidatsa Indians traveled was decidedly different from that which they would be employing.

Lewis and Clark were not, however, the type to dwell on such things. Recognizing that a decision had to be made, the captains set about gathering the facts. First, they climbed the bluffs to gather visual intelligence. The view to the south was clear and unobstructed and offered a magnificent panorama. It was evident the south fork flowed in from a southwesterly direction. Although

The Junction of the Marias and Missouri Rivers

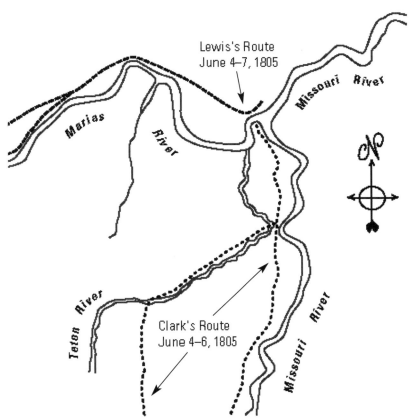

the northern view was blocked by hills, what little of the river they could see appeared to flow in from a westerly direction. All in all, the climb did not shed much new light on the situation.

Next, they set about measuring the width and depth of both rivers. They took the temperature, timed the speed of the current, and probed the beds of the river bottoms.

The north fork was deeper and similar in color and character to the Missouri, which is to say it was muddy and had a "whitish

brown" color and a "boiling and rolling manner." The south fork
ran faster, and its water was much clearer and had "a smooth
unriffled surface." Lewis added that it had "round and flat smooth
stones like most rivers issuing from a mountainous country."

The characteristics of the north fork were so similar to the
look and feel of the Missouri River—the river they had been traveling since they left Camp Dubois thirteen months earlier. Private
Joseph Whitehouse wrote in his journal, "Our officers and all the
men differ in [their] opinion of which river to take." Lewis sec-
onded this opinion by noting that if he and Clark were to give
their opinions they would "be the minority."

This meant that the two leaders were on the verge of making
the most momentous decision of the trip, and yet they were in disagreement with everyone else! The co-commanders' thinking was
logical. They felt that any river emanating from the mountains
would be clearer and run faster, and they had been told by the
Hidatsa that the Missouri ran clear at the Great Falls. These characteristics matched the south fork, and thus, they reasoned, the
south fork was the true Missouri.

The expedition was a military expedition and Lewis and Clark
were its leaders. At this point, the captains could have simply
announced their decision and ordered the team to proceed up the
south fork. To their credit, they did not do this. Having already
covered well over 2,000 miles, the expedition was functioning well
as a team and morale was high. To have completely disregarded
the opinions of every person in the group would have risked a
serious setback in the esprit de corps of the unit. Furthermore,
given the significance of the decision, the captains realized additional information was needed.

Lewis and Clark therefore dispatched separate teams up each
fork. Sergeant Nathaniel Pryor led his group up the north fork and

Sergeant Patrick Gass led another up the south fork. Pryor returned to report that the north fork, after flowing west for ten miles, eventually turned north. Gass returned to report the south fork took on a more southwesterly direction six miles down the river.

The results were inconclusive. In Lewis's words, the findings were "by no means satisfactory as to the fundamental point." There was only one thing to do. Lewis and Clark had to go out into the field themselves. They were the leaders of the expedition, and this was a decision that was vital to the expedition's success. President Thomas Jefferson's orders had been explicit: "The object of your mission is to explore the Missouri River." The task of determining which fork was the true Missouri could not be delegated. The success of the entire expedition rested squarely on the shoulders of Lewis and Clark and their ability to make the correct decision.

Lewis took the assignment of exploring the north fork and Clark went up the south. Both men selected small teams to assist them. For Lewis and his team, the walk was extremely difficult. They endured prickly pears and were drenched by a cold, hard rain. Still they covered thirty-two miles the first day and thirty miles the next. On the morning of the third day, approximately seventy miles upriver, Lewis finally came to the conclusion "that this branch of the Missouri had its direction too much to the north" to lead to the headwaters of the Missouri. He had made his decision.

Meanwhile to the south, Captain Clark followed the other fork for a day and a half before concluding that the river "continued its width, debth & rapidity and the Course west of South" and was therefore the true Missouri.

Now came the difficult part—convincing their team that they had made the correct decision. According to Lewis's journal entry of June 9, 1805, the men were firm in their belief that the north fork was the true Missouri and that it was the one they should follow.

Even Pierre Cruzatte, the expedition's most skilled boatman and best navigator, "declared it as his opinion that the [north] fork was the true genuine Missouri and could be no other."

To the men of the expedition, who had only known the Missouri River—and before that the Mississippi River—to be muddy and brown, it was logical to conclude that because the Marias was also brown and muddy, it must therefore be the Missouri. It was the equivalent of someone saying, "It has always been this way, so it must always be." They were blinded by their past experience.

Lewis and Clark, however, by exploring all the facts and going into the field themselves, were confident enough of their decision to overcome the objections of their team. Thus, on the morning of June 9, they announced their decision and endeavored "to impress on the minds of the party" the belief that the north fork was the Missouri. In a testimonial to their extraordinary leadership skills, Lewis recorded that the men were "very cheerfully [and] ready to follow us any wher[e] we thought proper." He added, however, "that they still thought that the other was the river."

On June 13, Lewis, with great joy, received the confirmation that he had expected—he heard a "roaring too tremendious to be mistaken for any cause short of the Great Falls of the Missouri." It was confirmation that he and William Clark had made the right decision—a decision that was strengthened by their willingness to lead and go up the rivers themselves and take responsibility for the unpopular decision.

Finding the Shoshone

After reaching the Great Falls and discovering there was not one waterfall but five, and realizing that the expected half-day portage would actually take nearly a month, the captains began to become concerned. It had been almost three months since they left Fort Mandan; the days were now getting shorter and they were nowhere near the headwaters of the Missouri. If they were going to reach the Pacific before winter, they needed to find the Shoshone, with whom they were to trade for horses to meet their transportation needs.

Anxious to locate them, the captains agreed that Clark and a small party would move ahead in search of the Indians. The captains were reluctant to separate and weaken their party, especially in a territory where hostile Indians might be present, but, as with the decision at the Marias, they had reached another critical juncture in their journey and it was their responsibility to guide the expedition to success. Clark ventured out and returned a few days later, unsuccessful.

By mid-July, the expedition had slowed to a crawl. The Missouri River was getting shallower and navigation was slow and cumbersome. If they were going to succeed, it was imperative that they locate the elusive Shoshone. The situation was nearing the desperation point. The nights were growing colder, and food was becoming scarcer.

Again, the captains agreed that one of them needed to go out in search of the Indians. Still suffering from bruised and bloodied feet from his earlier trip, Clark set out. Again, he returned unsuccessful.

August was now approaching and still there was no sign of the Shoshone. Lewis wrote: "We begin to feel considerable anxiety with respect to the [Shoshone] . . . If we do not find them . . . I fear the successfull issue of our voyage will be very doubtful." He then added that without the benefit of the Shoshones' knowledge, the Corps of Discovery would have no idea how far the mountains continued, where the best pass was, or even where to hook up with the Columbia River on the other side of the mountains. They were headed straight into the most difficult part of their journey, and they were essentially blind.

In early August, Lewis took over from Clark and went out in search of the Shoshone. For the first week he was unsuccessful, but he was not about to quit. In his journal he resolved to find the Indians even "if it should cause me a trip of one month." So serious was the situation that Lewis, for the only known time in the expedition, left written instructions in the event that he should die. He was prepared to do whatever it took to succeed.

On August 11, Lewis finally spotted an Indian on horseback. He was elated. The young Shoshone warrior, however, was frightened off by the presence of Lewis's small team. It was the worst possible result. The Indian would likely return to his tribe to warn them of a war party. The tribe, in turn, could be expected to mount a war party of their own.

In spite of this new danger, Lewis knew he had no choice but to proceed. On August 12, 1805, the importance of finding the Shoshone became a critical matter. For it was on this day that he reached the Continental Divide, the point at which he had expected to find a river flowing westward from the western side of the divide, and saw only more mountains. Without horses, the Corps of Discovery would most certainly be unable to succeed in crossing further. Luckily, the next day, the long search finally ended. Lewis came across three Shoshone women in a field and convinced them of his peaceful intentions.

The captains' persistence and willingness to lead from the front and do what was necessary to locate the Shoshone set the stage for the next portion of their journey: the trip over the Bitterroot Mountains.

"Those Tremendous Mountains"

In early September 1805, as the Corps of Discovery descended into the Bitterroot Valley (located between the borders of western Montana and eastern Idaho), they encountered 400 Salish Indians at a place called Ross' Hole. The Salish, who were subsisting on nothing more than berries and roots, were moving east to hunt buffalo.

After trading for some horses, the two groups went in separate directions—the Salish toward the eastern plains, which were rich with game, and the Corps of Discovery west toward the snow-covered mountains, which possessed only the most meager supplies of edible food. The captains' decision to proceed westward can only be categorized as pure, unadulterated courage.

For the next few days the expedition continued some sixty miles through the relatively flat valley and made good progress. Constantly looming to their immediate left were the mountains. Patrick Gass wrote they were "the most terrible mountains I have ever beheld."

Eventually, the Corps of Discovery reached a place called Traveler's Rest, near present-day Lolo Creek, Idaho, and prepared for their assault of the Bitterroot mountain range. Lewis wrote that virtually every Indian, save for their guide—an Indian known as Old Toby—believed the passage "impractical."

With nothing but courage, they advanced up the ominous mountain range. The most difficult stage of the journey began on September 11. A few days later, they were in the thick of the dense mountain brush. Clark wrote, "[T]he road through this hilley Country is verry bad passing over hills & thro' Steep hollows, over falling timber . . . [and] the Sides of Steep Strong mountains." Through rain, hail, and snow they continued. At one point, Old

Toby made a mistake and the group became lost for a few days. So famished were the men that they had to kill a colt for food.

Still, they proceeded over the mountains. On September 16, more snow fell and the footing was so treacherous that a few horses slipped down the steep hills. The thick, wet, heavy snow caused Clark to write, "I have been wet and cold in every part as I ever was in my life." He even feared his feet were about to freeze through his thin moccasins. That evening, the members were even wetter, colder, hungrier, and more exhausted than they were the previous day. The trees were so numerous and thick and the ground so rugged that they could scarcely find a level patch of earth on which to lay their wet blankets. The Corps of Discovery had hit rock bottom. Exhausted, reduced to eating candles, and seeing no relief from the mountains, Lewis and Clark knew they needed to provide their team with some hope.

For the third time in almost as many months, they recognized it was necessary to split up and send one of them ahead. It was decided that Clark would lead a small party in search of food and Indians. This time, he was successful. Within two days he found the Nez Percé Indians, from whom he procured some dried fish and roots, then he dispatched a man back to deliver the supplies—which helped sustain the party on their last leg through the mountains. On September 22, eleven days and 165 miles after they first entered the mountains of the Bitterroot Range, the Corps of Discovery dragged themselves into a Nez Percé village. Their perilous ordeal was over.

Whether Lewis and Clark's decision to separate in the Bitterroots was ultimately essential to their survival is debatable. What is not debatable is that just as they did in the confrontation with the Teton Sioux, at the critical juncture at the Marias, and in their search for the Shoshone, the captains took control of the situation, put themselves at the front, and assumed complete responsibility for the success of the mission. When situations required tough decisions, they made them; when the danger was the greatest, they placed themselves in harm's way; and when the success of the mission was hanging in the balance, Lewis and Clark always led from the front.

Leading Into the Unknown

In all likelihood, business leaders will not be presented with the same life-and-death situations as Lewis and Clark, but there are still a great many practical lessons of "leading from the front" that today's executives can take away from the captain's experiences.

Stand your ground. In their confrontation with the Sioux, Lewis and Clark knew that to give in to the tribe's demands for more trading goods would have placed them in a weakened position vis-à-vis other Indian tribes further upstream with whom they still had to trade. Furthermore, to appease the Sioux would have been to give in to intimidation. Their situation was in some ways analogous to a large business customer who expects or demands greater service at the expense of smaller customers. The temptation to give in (while understandable because of the prominence of the client) could weaken a company's ability to build stronger relationships with smaller clients who may grow into larger clients in the future. Moreover, once a company develops a pattern of providing preferential treatment, it only encourages the recipient to make repeat demands.

In his book *Leadership*, Rudy Giuliani dedicates an entire chapter to "standing up to bullies." Although he has many wonderful examples, he starts with his efforts as mayor of New York City to get United Nations diplomats to pay their parking tickets. He felt it was necessary to stand up to people who didn't think they had to play by the rules. Taking a stance similar to Lewis and Clark's with the Teton Sioux, Giuliani felt that to give in would only encourage more flagrant violations.

Put yourself in the line of fire. In the confrontation with the Teton Sioux, William Clark did not retreat, and he did not hesitate to express his displeasure directly to the offensive Indian chief. He stood his ground and spoke directly to him. It is the equivalent of an executive delivering a tough message directly to a client. While it is possible to delegate the responsibility, executives who tackle the situation themselves establish an aura of authority that can enhance their respect in the eyes of both clients and employees. Both outcomes can have positive implications for future events.

As a tangible example, I cite the former CEO of Johnson & Johnson, James Burke, and his courageous action in the face of the 1982 Tylenol tampering scare when seven people were poisoned to death. In addition to immediately pulling the product from all stores across the country (at a cost of nearly a billion dollars), Burke faced the public by going on "Donahue" and "60 Minutes" to answer all questions. Contrast this with former Exxon CEO Lawrence G. Rawl and his behavior in the aftermath of the *Exxon Valdez* fiasco, when he dispatched two lower-level executives to Alaska to deal with the situation, instead of managing the situation himself. The actions of leaders at moments of crisis send strong signals to everyone involved—be they customers, employees, or the public—and can produce both immediate and longer-term results.

Go into the field yourself. At the crucial decision at the Marias, Lewis and Clark first dispatched two of their sergeants. When they came back with inconclusive evidence, the captains knew it was their responsibility to go out into the field. The success of the mission was their responsibility; it could not be delegated. This is a lesson that is extremely appropriate for today's executives. How many times is an executive presented with a choice between two paths? They can rely on consultants. But, like the Indians who didn't even know about the Marias River's existence, consultants can be wrong. They can also confer with their employees. But just as with Pierre Cruzatte, the master boatman who had only known rivers to be brown and muddy, the employee's perspective may be limited to his or her past experience. As a leader, it is the executive's responsibility to gather as much information as possible and analyze it. When that analysis does not lead to a clear decision, the executive must go out into the field.

Go with your gut. In the end, Lewis and Clark, even after going out into the field and gathering as much information as was possible, still had to fall back on their gut instincts to make their final decision. The decision, which ran counter to the opinions of everyone in their group, was similar to Akio Morita's decision when he was chairman of Sony Corporation to push ahead with the development of the Sony Walkman. As he later recounted, he just knew it was the right decision. And when he said, "If we had failed with the Walkman, I could not have pointed to any market research as the cause of the fiasco," what he was really saying was that he was prepared to accept absolute responsibility for the decision. But, like Lewis and Clark, he didn't have to, because he made the right decision.

Remember, with responsibility comes more responsibility. Once Lewis and Clark made the decision at the Marias, their responsibility was not done. They still needed to communicate the rationale behind the decision. In many ways, what happens after a decision is made in any business is as important as actually making the decision. Lewis and Clark, like good bosses, not only clearly communicated the decision, they also outlined all the issues leading up to the decision, described the key elements used in making the decision, and explained how the decision was going to be implemented.

Persist in the face of adversity. The Shoshone were critical to the Corps of Discovery's success, and Lewis and Clark knew they had no choice but to find them. In a sense, the Shoshone situation would be analogous to finding new customers during an economic downturn: If a business can't find them, the enterprise may perish. The lesson of Lewis and Clark's experience is that in critical situations, the responsibility for delivering success rests with the leader. It is not something that can be delegated. As Lewis and Clark demonstrated when they were unsuccessful the first three times they ventured out, persistence is the key. Only when Lewis vowed to stay out a whole month did he succeed. The business lesson—which can't be reiterated enough—is that 90 percent of the results often come from the final 10 percent of effort.

Do something. In the Bitterroot Mountains, the situation was desperate. There was some logic to keeping the group together, but at that point what the Corps of Discovery really needed was hope. Although there were better hunters and more skilled trackers who could have led the advance scouting mission, Clark decided to lead the group. His example reminds us that at the end of the day, it is the responsibility of the leader not only to provide hope, but to actively deliver it when necessary. The members of the Corps of Discovery, like employees, were probably more willing to continue forward and risk possible death because they knew their leaders were doing everything in their power to get them out of a bad situation as quickly as possible.

In 2001, in the wake of the terrorist attacks, most airlines were forced to lay off 20 percent or more of their workforce. Southwest Airlines refused to concede. Instead, its leaders searched out new markets that the other airlines had abandoned and its employees responded by voluntarily taking pay cuts, forgoing profit sharing, and donating their time. Southwest survived without having to lay off a single employee because the company's leaders and employees responded with tangible action.

Proceed On!

In 1968, Swiss watchmakers controlled 80 percent of the world market for high-quality watches. By 1973, their share had plummeted to less than 25 percent and 50,000 watchmakers were out of jobs. Confronted with a fork in the road in the late 1960s, Swiss watchmakers had to choose between adopting new quartz technology or staying with the old standard. They assumed that consumers would continue to prefer handmade, mechanical watches over quartz watches. Could the outcome have been prevented? It likely could have—especially if the executives had gone out into the field to understand both the emerging technology and the needs of their customers.

The Swiss watchmakers were not unique in their mistake. In the 1980s, the supercomputer industry failed to understand the impact of the personal computer, and Motorola, Inc. repeated the mistake in the late 1990s with regard to its decision initially to stay with analog technology instead of switching to digital technology. By the time Motorola finally made the change, its market share had decreased significantly.

It is likely that the same thing will happen to companies in this decade—only it will occur on a greater scale. Fuel cells and solar cells are threatening to revolutionize the energy industry; new medical treatments will disrupt the medical and pharmaceutical industries; and new manufacturing methods are transforming many older, traditional industries.

It is easy to dismiss such projections—much as the men of the Corps of Discovery dismissed the idea that the south fork was the true Missouri because it didn't conform to their thinking. However, business executives—by analyzing trends, looking at things from as many different perspectives as possible, getting out into the field, and persisting in the face of adversity—can accurately assess which direction is true for their companies. But first they must accept the fact that the task is one of their primary responsibilities.

CHAPTER SEVEN

MEANINGFUL MENTORING
The Principle of Learning from Others

There are two ways to acquire wisdom; you can either buy it or borrow it. By buying it, you pay full price in terms of time and cost to learn the lessons you need to learn. By borrowing it, you go to those men and women who have already paid the price to learn the lessons and get their wisdom from them.

—Benjamin Franklin

The concept of mentoring goes back to ancient Athens. The term *mentor* comes directly from Homer's *The Odyssey*, in which the character Mentor was a tutor and guide to Telemachus during his travels in search of his father, Odysseus. Ultimately, the father and son were successfully reunited, and over the centuries the word *mentor* has come to mean trusted adviser, teacher, friend, and wise person. I start with this story because just as Mentor was instrumental to Telemachus's success, mentoring was equally important to the success of the Lewis and Clark expedition, which has been called the "American Odyssey."

The effect of mentoring on Lewis and Clark was both significant and subtle. An example of the latter occurred on February 11, 1805, when Sacagawea, the young Indian teenager who accompanied Lewis and Clark on their expedition, gave birth to a baby boy, Jean Baptiste Charbonneau ("Pomp"). In his journal for the day, Meriwether Lewis, who was caring for Sacagawea during her birth, wrote:

[I]t is worthy of remark that this was the first child which this woman had boarn and as is common in such cases her labour was tedious and the pain violent; Mr. Jessome [Rene Jessaume was a French trader who had lived with the Mandans for years] informed me that he had frequently administered a small portion of the rattle of the rattlesnake, which he assured me had never failed to produce the desired effect, that of hastening the birth of the child; having the rattle of a snake by me I gave it to him and he administered two rings of it to the woman broken in small pieces with the fingers and added to a small quantity of water. Whether this medicine was truly the cause or not I shall not undertake to determine, but I was informed that she had not taken it more than ten minutes before she brought forth; perhaps this remedy may be worthy of future experiments, but I must confess that I want faith as to [its] efficacy.

It is a revealing passage because in the last sentence, Lewis appears at once open to the possibility that the rattles may have had a positive medicinal effect on Sacagawea, but also skeptical. As a man of the Enlightenment, he wanted further proof. This "open-minded skepticism"[1] was one of the many characteristics that contributed to Lewis and Clark's success by keeping them flexible and open to new approaches. The passage is also illuminating because Lewis relied on the advice of two different mentors in considering the result. Specifically, he relied on the early training he received from his mother during his childhood, and on the wisdom of Thomas Jefferson, who taught him to be curious, skeptical, and open-minded all at the same time. These experiences encapsulate the seventh leadership principle of Lewis and Clark, meaningful mentoring: the principle of learning from others.

Early Influences: Family, the Plantation, and the Military

Meriwether Lewis's first instructor was his mother, Lucy Meriwether Marks. She was a skilled herb doctor who understood the medicinal properties of various plants and passed this knowledge on to her son. It was this knowledge, in part, that allowed him to accept the possibility that the rattles from snakes might somehow help induce birth. From her Lewis also learned the basics of reading, writing, and arithmetic. William Clark received similar instruction from his brother, George Rogers Clark.

The preponderance of the captains' practical skills, however, were obtained through what Stephen Ambrose called "the school of the plantation." By this he meant that Lewis and Clark, by virtue of being plantation owners, were knowledgeable about soils and crops and trained in a variety of areas such as blacksmithing, carpentry, herding, butchering, and shoemaking.

Most of these practical skills were honed—and some new ones acquired—while Lewis and Clark were serving as military officers in the frontier army. During these years, both Lewis and

Clark also had the opportunity to serve under General Anthony Wayne. Although his influence on both men has not been accorded much attention by historians, it was Wayne who chose not to court-martial Meriwether Lewis early in his career, when Lewis got drunk and challenged another officer to a duel. Wayne's decision, which ran counter to the existing code of military justice at the time, likely shaped Lewis's own approach to discipline, which, as we saw in Chapter Five, was equally flexible. The decision also changed history because had Lewis been court-martialed, it is unlikely he would have been considered for a command as important as that of leading the Corps of Discovery. And in one of history's luckiest coincidences, the decision also resulted in Lewis's being transferred to William Clark's command, where the two men began their famous friendship.

General Wayne's patient and deliberate preparation as a military commander also had a lasting impact on William Clark. As a young officer, Clark was initially critical of Wayne's slow, deliberate, and methodical approach to warfare, but when he saw how it resulted in a decisive victory at the Battle of Fallen Timbers (a historic battle in which the U.S. Army defeated a confederation of Native American tribes and some British volunteers and paved the way for the United States to settle the Northwest Territory and expand beyond the original thirteen colonies), he came to appreciate the importance of training, preparation, and logistics.[2] During the expedition to the Pacific, Clark demonstrated that he had learned the lessons well.

During their time in the military, Lewis and Clark also gained a deep understanding of the geography of the land and learned firsthand the capabilities of the Indians. As officers, they received rudimentary medical training and learned how to set broken bones, fix dislocated joints, and treat basic ailments such as dysentery and venereal disease. They received valuable training in engineering and construction, intelligence gathering, diplomacy, and, of course, fighting and managing soldiers. Above all else, however, they learned to be flexible enough to change with conditions.

These practical skills, combined with the wisdom they acquired from their families, their military careers, and General Wayne, were helpful to the Corps of Discovery's survival. However, it was the instruction and advice from two very influential mentors that allowed Lewis and Clark to grow and prosper on the new frontier. In Meriwether Lewis's case, his mentor was Thomas Jefferson. William Clark's mentor was his older brother, George Rogers Clark.

Thomas Jefferson as Mentor

To understand Thomas Jefferson's importance as a mentor, it is important to understand that he himself was the product of mentors. His father, Peter Jefferson, as well as Peyton Randolph, a Virginia legislator, and, most important, George Wythe, an influential professor and prominent attorney, all greatly influenced him. This pattern of mentoring is one that Jefferson would continue. In addition to Meriwether Lewis, Jefferson also served as a mentor to both James Madison and James Monroe. Through Madison and Monroe, Jefferson continued to influence affairs in the White House for sixteen years after he left office.[3] Jefferson understood that to act as a mentor was to extend one's own influence.

Lewis received all of his mentoring from Jefferson during the two years he served as the president's personal secretary. During this time, he interacted with Jefferson on a daily basis, and it affected everything from his writing to his thinking. Jefferson was the leading Enlightenment thinker of his day. His heroes were

Francis Bacon, John Locke, and Isaac Newton, and it is from these political philosophers that Jefferson's influence must first be understood. He believed, above all else, in the cause of liberty.

The pursuit of liberty—and the expansion of the United States so that other peoples could pursue it—was, Jefferson believed, the primary purpose of government. It is a belief he helped instill in Lewis.

Jefferson's vision of the country—a country that stretched from coast to coast—also served to inspire Lewis. As the drafter of the Northwest Ordinance (a document in many ways as important as the Declaration of Independence because it provided a means for populated territories to become states),[4] Jefferson provided the rationale for exploring the land west of the Mississippi. It was needed to secure future territory for America.

Beyond these broad philosophical underpinnings, Jefferson, as a mentor, had a number of other practical influences on Meriwether Lewis. For instance, as the founder of America's first public university, the University of Virginia, and as the state's first politician to introduce legislation creating public education, Jefferson was a lifelong advocate of education. He believed that the future of democracy required the citizenry to be educated, and he viewed it as government's proper role to facilitate that education. At the same time, Jefferson also believed that students were responsible for their own learning. It is a lesson that Lewis took to heart. While at the White House and Monticello, Lewis also had the run of Jefferson's extensive library (which before Jefferson donated it to the federal government—where it became the foundation for the Library of Congress—contained the largest selection of books on the American West anywhere in the world) and made good use of it.

Directly tied to Jefferson's belief in education was the notion that with the right tools and information, a path could be charted through any wilderness. In essence, he believed that leadership could be learned. To this end, Jefferson set forth and worked to ensure that Lewis had the appropriate reservoir of knowledge to handle the many scientific and technical responsibilities for leading the Corps of Discovery. He did this by sending Lewis to Philadelphia to be tutored by some of America's brightest men of the day in the fields of science, natural history, and medicine.

Lewis started his rigorous crash course by meeting with the noted astronomer and mathematician Andrew Ellicott, who tutored him in mapmaking and surveying skills. Ellicott also worked with Lewis on his celestial navigation skills, which were essential for determining longitude and latitude and thus critical to accurate mapmaking. Lewis received additional navigational training from Robert Patterson and studied natural history and botany with Benjamin Barton Smith, who helped him learn how to identify and label plants. Caspar Wistar instructed him in anatomy and fossil identification, and he studied medicine with the preeminent physician of the day, Benjamin Rush. All told, Lewis's three months in Philadelphia were the equivalent of a graduate education. By all accounts, Lewis passed with flying colors.

The experience was critical to the expedition's success because Lewis employed the various skills on an almost daily basis. One of the side benefits of this crash course was that it was multidisciplinary in nature and introduced Lewis to the benefits of cross-pollination of ideas. Insights in one field of science led to an improved, deeper, or entirely new understanding in another area of science. For instance, the botany lessons increased his understanding of the medical properties of various plants, which, in turn, improved his doctoring skills.

There is ample evidence to suggest that Thomas Jefferson influenced Meriwether Lewis in a variety of other ways, too.

Jefferson was constantly reaching out to people of different experiences to learn new things. The invitation lists to his dinner parties were filled with scientists, writers, and people of all different ages, backgrounds, and experiences. As a frequent guest himself, Lewis would have undoubtedly been exposed to their ideas and experiences.

Jefferson was also not above seeking counsel from the best experts of his day. He was humble enough to ask questions, on subjects ranging from gardening to geopolitics, of those he believed had more experience than he. It was a practice that Lewis similarly employed in hiring boatmen and interpreters, and when listening to the Indians. Jefferson taught him that the truly smart person knows how much he doesn't know—and isn't afraid to ask others to teach him.

The president's belief in "a natural aristocracy, grounded in virtue and talents" also positively influenced Lewis. Jefferson believed in selecting people on the basis of merit. After becoming president, Jefferson wanted to reduce the size of the Army and ordered Lewis (whom he hired for this specific purpose) to identify the worthiness of all the officers. By virtue of his own Army experience, Lewis was eminently qualified for the task. John Adams, Jefferson's predecessor, had filled the officer ranks with partisan appointments. It would have been easy for Jefferson to simply ask Lewis to remove only those officers whose politics were different from his own. To his credit, Jefferson reduced the ranks according to each officer's soldiering skills. It was a lesson that Lewis and Clark followed in selecting their own men for the expedition.

It would not have been unrealistic to assume that Lewis, as a frontier Army officer, would view Indians as "savages." However, Thomas Jefferson's belief that the Indian was "in body and mind equal to the white man" likely positively affected Lewis's dealing with the natives. The result was that Lewis had remarkable success in his dealings with Indians because he viewed them, with minor exceptions, as individuals worthy of respect.

Jefferson's preference for diplomacy over war is yet another area where Jefferson exerted subtle influence on Lewis. Before the Louisiana Purchase, the Federalists were calling for a war with France to secure the Port of New Orleans. Jefferson recognized that for the cost of a war, the United States might instead be able to simply buy the port. In the end, Jefferson's handpicked negotiators came away with a much better deal. For $15 million, or a mere three cents an acre, he doubled the size of America—without firing a single shot or losing one American life. In so doing, he helped secure the country from foreign invasion and set it on a path to become a superpower. Jefferson always looked to diplomacy first—not because he was a pacifist, but because he viewed it as the most efficient and effective means of achieving his goals. On numerous occasions on their journey, Lewis and Clark both employed similar thinking.

Even Jefferson's writing style influenced Lewis. Jefferson's book, *Notes on the State of Virginia*, is said to have served as a template for Lewis's own recording of his findings on the plants and wildlife he encountered on the expedition.

But perhaps Jefferson's greatest influence on Meriwether Lewis was just being at his side as he prepared for the journey. Jefferson was constantly envisioning what the land to the west might hold. As a result, this led to a series of questions, and these questions helped Lewis prepare for the journey.

Jefferson's detailed instructions to Lewis are telling because there was virtually nothing the president wasn't interested in, and his inherent curiosity was imparted to his young protégé. For instance, according to his instructions, Jefferson wanted to know "the names of the nations & their numbers; the extent & limits of their possessions; their relations with other tribes or nations; their language . . . occupations in agriculture, fishing, hunting, war [and] arts . . . the soil & face of the country; [its] growth & vegetable productions . . . the animal of the country generally . . . the mineral productions of every kind. . . ." He concluded his instructions with an order to record the "climate as characterized by the thermometer, by proportion of rainy, cloudy & clear days, by [lightning], hail, snow, ice, by the access & recess of frost, by the winds prevailing at different seasons, the dates at which particular plants put forth or lose their flowers, or leaf, times of appearances of particular birds, reptiles or insects." In short, there was almost nothing that the president didn't want to know, and Jefferson's curiosity buttressed Lewis's own curiosity.

George Rogers Clark as Mentor

Thomas Jefferson was close friends with George Rogers Clark, William Clark's older brother. In fact, in 1783, when Jefferson was vice president of the American Philosophical Society, he led an effort to privately raise the funds necessary to send an American expedition by land to the Pacific Ocean. The first person to whom he turned to lead the expedition was George Rogers Clark. While flattered and supportive of the cause, Clark turned him down, saying that he was not in a position to lead such an expedition at the time.

I recount the story because it demonstrates that Jefferson believed Clark's older brother possessed all the prerequisites to successfully head an expedition and that as his younger brother's primary mentor, George Rogers Clark undoubtedly imparted many of these same skills to William.

Unlike William, George Clark had some formal education and received training in Greek, Latin, literature, philosophy, history, and medicine. He was also familiar with Enlightenment thinkers such as Hume, Locke, and Voltaire. This is important because it suggests that William Clark received some instruction from his older brother and thus was well versed in many different areas and not the simple backwoods man that he is sometimes portrayed to be. Both Lewis and Clark were "Renaissance men" in the true sense of the word, and their mentors encouraged their interest in a wide variety of intellectual pursuits.

George Rogers Clark held a particularly deep interest in science and natural history. In fact, he said of himself, "I don't suppose there is a person living that knows the geography and natural history of the back [country] better if so well as I do myself . . . it has been my study for years."[5] All of this knowledge he shared with his little brother.

That George Rogers Clark was a great military leader is also well documented. Charismatic and bold, he was said to have established great rapport with his men. He conquered one fort without firing a shot, and in another battle, he beat a much larger and better-equipped army by making a daring midwinter raid and bluffing his opponents into thinking the size of his force was four times what it actually was.

Like Jefferson, George Rogers Clark also preferred diplomacy over war, especially with the Indians. One story tells of him offering the Indians "the red belt of war" or the "white belt of peace." The Indians chose the latter. His respect for the Indians was also evident in the fact that after he retired, George Clark was held in such esteem by Indian chiefs and warriors that many continued to visit with him at his home to smoke "the pipe of peace." William Clark's genuine affection for Indians—which was well documented by his post-expedition career—was undoubtedly shaped by his brother's similar affection toward the Indians.

Unlike Jefferson's relationship with Lewis, little else is known about the relationship between the Clark brothers. But so great was William Clark's respect for his brother that it has been said that when he was older, William was reluctant to discuss his many accomplishments but rarely declined the opportunity to recount the heroics of his older brother. Given the brothers' similarities in leadership style, and their preference for diplomacy over war and good relations with the Indians, it is clear that William Clark did more than just take the stories to heart; he actively tried to emulate his brother—and did so to great effect.

Leading Into the Unknown

It is difficult to ascertain the extent to which Lewis and Clark actively courted their mentors, but one story stands out to suggest that Meriwether Lewis understood how important Thomas Jefferson could be to his future. In 1793, ten years before he authorized the Corps of Discovery's expedition, Jefferson, as a member of the American Philosophical Society, helped raise money to fund a similar expedition. He ultimately hired a French botanist by the name of Andre Michaux (this first attempted expedition failed when Jefferson recalled Michaux after learning he was a French spy).[6] The story is important because there is evidence that suggests that Lewis, although only eighteen years old at the time, applied for the position but was apparently turned down—most likely because of his age. The story is important because it is my personal opinion that Lewis then spent the better part of the next ten years working to put himself in a position to lead Jefferson's next attempt. Moreover, it suggests that Lewis understood that Jefferson might be able to assist him on both a practical and an intellectual level. Not only could Jefferson open doors for him, he could also provide Lewis with the necessary skills to succeed once the door was opened. In short, Lewis understood the value of having Thomas Jefferson as a mentor.

The story also illustrates the four characteristics to look for when selecting a mentor:

Choose people you respect, admire, and want to emulate. From their earliest years, it is evident that both Lewis and Clark looked up to their respective mentors. Thomas Jefferson and George Rogers Clark were both men of integrity and honor, and their behavior mirrored their convictions. When searching for a mentor, it is important to select someone who not only possesses the knowledge and experience you want and need, but also can teach you by his example.

Look for someone who genuinely wants you to succeed. This advice might sound obvious, but good mentors must believe in what their protégé is hoping to accomplish. Thomas Jefferson and George Rogers Clark both understood what a successful mission would mean to America, so they were committed to its success. Good mentors also realize that they too benefit from the relationship. Mentors have an opportunity to continue to learn from those younger than themselves; at the same time, the mentoring relationship offers them an opportunity to expand their influence. In Jefferson's case, he cemented his legacy as a visionary, westward-looking president.

Look for criticism, not praise. For the mentor-protégé relationship to work, the protégé must be open to being influenced. This means that they must be open to constructive criticism. As the old saying goes, praise only reinforces what you know; criticism forces you to learn more. Thomas Jefferson's suggestion that Lewis study in Philadelphia indicates that he was not shy about informing his protégé about the areas where he felt Lewis was deficient.

Look for mentors with a breadth of experience and perspective. Neither Thomas Jefferson nor George Rogers Clark was an explorer in the true sense of the word, yet both men possessed so many other unique skills and experiences that their collective wisdom could be applied to many different situations. Good mentors should understand their protégés' business, but they should also bring a fresh, outside perspective that can shed a new or different light on existing situations.

The chances that a person will be lucky enough to find mentors of the skill and capability of Thomas Jefferson or George Rogers Clark are remote, but the important thing to remember is that mentors must be sought out. As rare as Jefferson was, it is even more rare that a mentor will just come to you. One company that is taking an innovative approach to mentoring is Instill Corporation, a business-to-business company in the food service industry, located in Redwood City, California. The company has established an extensive mentorship program as part of its leadership grooming process. All senior executives are asked to select a mentor they admire, someone from whom they think they can learn. These executives, more often than not, work at another company. The mentors must then be approved by the company's board. In exchange for their commitment to serve as mentors, they are offered stock in the company. Since the program was started in 1998, no mentor approached by an Instill executive has yet refused the opportunity to participate, and the program is reported to be a great success.[7]

The Benefits of Meaningful Mentoring

Lewis and Clark's experiences highlight six benefits that protégés can expect to derive from a meaningful mentor relationship.

Mentors can expand your horizon. Thomas Jefferson helped Meriwether Lewis understand that the mission was not just about commerce; it was about nation building and the Manifest Destiny of America. And George Rogers Clark, a veteran war hero, undoubtedly understood that a successful mission meant America could assert its control over the North American continent and, as such, likely encouraged his younger brother to accept the invitation to co-lead the project.

Ben Lytle, former chairman, president, and CEO of Anthem Insurance Company (and now chairman emeritus), speaks of his career in terms of a series of mentors. His mother and sister fostered his creativity; a former division manager helped him manage his time better; and a CEO he worked for early in his career helped him develop new skills and encouraged him to take a different educational track, which was ultimately more beneficial to his career than the one he was planning on pursuing.[8]

Mentors can introduce you to other people who can further your career. Without Thomas Jefferson's assistance, Meriwether Lewis would not have been introduced to the most skilled and trained doctors, botanists, and astronomers of his day. Good mentors will similarly put their protégés in contact with people who can further their careers. David Packard and William Hewlett, the co-founders of Hewlett-Packard Company, are often credited with starting Silicon Valley's high-tech industry out of their garage in Palo Alto. The truth is that a man named Fred Terman is really the founder of Silicon Valley. A professor at Stanford University from the late 1930s through the 1970s, Terman served as a mentor to both Hewlett and Packard. As an instructor, he motivated the two men with his vision of the future and his "unique ability to make complex problems seem the essence of simplicity." Terman stressed the importance of multidisciplinary thinking and encouraged Hewlett and Packard to meet with other chemists, physicists, and electrical engineers in informal settings to share ideas. He also pushed the two men hard and forced them to constantly rethink their ideas and, when they felt they were right, to act on those ideas. In fact, it was Terman who prodded the men to start their own business. Perhaps most important, however, is that once they were in business, Terman went out of his way to introduce Hewlett and Packard to a wide network of powerful people in industry and government who were instrumental in growing their business.

Mentors can help you develop a new approach to your work. General Anthony Wayne's methodical approach to warfare, while difficult for the young and impatient William Clark to comprehend, eventually helped him understand the importance of training and preparation. Similarly, Jefferson's willingness to employ diplomacy first, rather than fighting, was instructive to Lewis. Good mentors will have a different and broader perspective. Or because they have made mistakes of their own in the past, they can help younger leaders view things differently, as well as reprioritize their many responsibilities.

Mentors serve as reality checkers. At one point during the winter of 1803, Meriwether Lewis considered using the winter months to go explore the New Mexico Territory. Jefferson immediately put an end to the idea by reminding Lewis that the purpose of his mission was much larger and the country could ill afford to lose him in a side trip that offered limited value. The situation is somewhat analogous to a businessperson who is looking to expand into a new business area. Good mentors, because of their experience, can help assess risk and identify potential threats and opportunities, as well as provide focus. If a decision appears to be ill conceived (as was Lewis's decision to explore New Mexico), a good mentor can point out the potential consequences.

Mentors set high expectations for performance. Thomas Jefferson fully expected Lewis and Clark to succeed. He gave them clear and detailed instructions and then ensured that they had the necessary training and funding to execute the mission. Not only must mentors set high expectations, they should also provide a realistic and often critical look at whether their protégés are meeting those expectations.

Mentors act as confidants and help build self-confidence. Good mentors, by their example and their advice, provide their protégés with the confidence to believe in themselves. They can listen to concerns and provide useful advice on how to minimize and/or eliminate concerns and problems. That Lewis and Clark never once doubted themselves and only expressed the greatest optimism can, in part, be attributed to the influence of Thomas Jefferson and George Rogers Clark.

Proceed On!

In conducting its research for *Fortune* magazine's "100 Best Companies to Work for in America," Hewitt Associates made some findings on mentoring. Among the highlights:

→ Of the companies surveyed, 77 percent found mentoring to be an effective tool to retain employees. (In fact, the study found that the presence or absence of mentoring was more critical than income in explaining job satisfaction.)

→ Of college graduates, 60 percent said mentoring played a role in choosing an employer.

→ Of executives surveyed, 75 percent said mentoring played a role in their career success.

→ Mentoring was one of three factors for Fortune 500 CEO success.[9]

Lewis and Clark, I believe, would not have been surprised by the results. They understood how important their mentors were to their success. In fact, William Clark once referred to Thomas Jefferson as "that great [character,] the Main Spring of the action." The praise stemmed from the fact that it was Jefferson who conceived the expedition, then authorized and funded its execution, and, through his historic act of diplomacy in which he acquired the Louisiana Territory, provided more meaning to the mission.

Yet it was no less Jefferson's own personal character that helped guide the Corps of Discovery to success. Jefferson once wrote:

If ever you find yourself environed with difficulties and perplexing circumstances out of which you are at a loss how to extricate yourself, do what is right, and be assured that that will extricate you the best out of the worst situations. Though you cannot see when you take one step what will be the next, yet follow truth, justice and plain dealing, and never fear leading you out of the labyrinth in the easiest manner possible . . . Be assured that nothing will be so pleasing as your success.

Such subtle guidance can often make the difference between success and failure; and business leaders of all ages and levels of seniority can benefit by acquiring the wisdom of those who have gone before them.

CHAPTER EIGHT

REALISTIC OPTIMISM
The Principle of Positive Thinking

An optimist sees an opportunity in every calamity; a pessimist sees a calamity in every opportunity.
—Winston Churchill

A leader is a dealer in hope.
—Napoleon Bonaparte

On May 26, 1805, more than a full year after the Corps of Discovery had left Camp Dubois and more than a month after they had departed from their winter headquarters at Fort Mandan, Meriwether Lewis went out late in the afternoon and hiked up some river hills. Upon reaching the summit of one of the higher hills, he looked out in the distance and saw what he thought were the Rocky Mountains for the first time. That evening he returned to camp and wrote the following in his journal:

[W]hile I viewed these mountains I felt a secret pleasure in finding myself so near the head of the heretofore conceived boundless Missouri; but when I reflected on the difficulties which this snowey barrier would most probably throw in my way to the Pacific, and the sufferings and hardships of myself and party in them, it in some measure counterbalanced the joy I had felt in the first moments in which I gazed upon them; but as I have always held it a crime to anticipate evils I will believe it a good comfortable road untill I am compelled to beleive differently.

The passage is a perfect illustration of Lewis and Clark's eighth leadership principle: realistic optimism. The first thing that the reader will notice in the passage is that Lewis emphasized the positive. He spoke about his "secret pleasure" and the "joy" he felt upon seeing the mountains. He did not focus on the negative. He did, however, in the very next phrase, offer a realistic assessment of the situation. He acknowledged the difficulties, sufferings, and hardships that he and the expedition would likely encounter because of the mountains. But then, in a phrase that I believe sums up both Lewis and Clark's optimistic outlook, he concluded with this assessment: "I will believe it a good comfortable road untill I am compelled to beleive differently." In essence, he was saying that until he was shown otherwise, he was going to assume that things would work out.

It is the classic profile of an optimist, and this particular trait was instrumental to the Corps of Discovery's success. For whenever it seemed as if things couldn't possibly get any worse, they did; but Lewis and Clark's consistently positive attitude helped the expedition proceed on in the expectation that better days were just ahead. And they would come to rely greatly on this optimism—for when Lewis penned the aforementioned passage, he wasn't even looking at the snow-capped peaks of the Rockies; he was actually viewing the Highwood Mountains. The much more treacherous terrain of the Rockies lay still further to the west.

Confident from the Beginning

The nature of Lewis and Clark's optimism is unknown. It is not known whether their fathers or mothers were inherently optimistic, whether the characteristic developed from a string of early successes in life, or if they just had the good fortune of being born with a positive disposition. All that is known is that their optimism was with them from the beginning of their journey.

In a letter to his mother in July 1803, just as he was beginning to prepare for the journey, Lewis wrote: "I feel myself perfectly prepared . . . I go with the most perfect preconviction in my own mind of returning safe." Thus, before he even set out, he had already visualized a successful mission and his safe return.

The point is an important one because, regardless of whether optimism is caused by a string of early successes, studies (some of which are discussed later in this chapter) have demonstrated that the reverse is definitely true. In other words, an optimistic outlook has been proven to lead to success.

In Lewis and Clark's case, their optimism was tested almost immediately. Not less than two months into the expedition, the Corps of Discovery suffered its first casualty. (It would also be the expedition's last casualty, though no one could have foreseen that at the time. Most members probably assumed more people would die over the course of the journey.) Shortly thereafter, a soldier went missing, and then the expedition experienced its first desertion. Thus, two months into the trip and heading into territory known to be occupied by the Sioux Indians, the Corps of Discovery had its ranks reduced by nearly 10 percent.

It would have been easy to view each successive setback as part of a much larger pattern—a pattern that was decidedly negative. Instead, Lewis and Clark chose to view each occurrence as an individual, isolated incident. Their optimism was rewarded as they found the missing soldier, captured the deserter, and survived the first leg of their journey.

"EVERYTHING TO HOPE"

As they prepared to leave their winter camp at Fort Mandan in April 1805, the expedition was about to set foot onto territory that, up until that time in history, no American had ever traversed. If they were confident up to this point, it could in part have been based on the knowledge that others had at least gone as far the Mandan villages. As they moved westward, this was no longer true. They stood on the edge of the unknown. Their map simply labeled the area "terra incognito." Still, neither Lewis nor Clark expressed any concern. Instead, Lewis continued to demonstrate his unrelenting optimism in both a letter to his mother and another one to President Jefferson.

On March 31, 1805, he wrote to his mother: "I feel the most perfect confidence that we shall reach the Pacific Ocean this summer." To the president he wrote: "I can foresee no material or probable obstruction to our progress, and entertain therefore the most sanguine hopes of complete success." He went on to add that everyone was in excellent health and anxious to proceed on. He concluded by saying that "[w]ith such men I have everything to hope, and but little to fear."

Some of his optimism undoubtedly stemmed from the fact that the Corps of Discovery had already successfully ventured more than 1,600 miles upriver. Some optimism may have come from the information he had gathered from the Indians over the winter, who communicated that the portage around the Great Falls would only be a half-day journey. All in all, however, there was no information that suggested the trek would be either easy or risk-free—that was simply how the captains chose to view the situation. Even in his journal on April 7, 1805—when he could no longer be accused of trying to "sugar coat" the situation for his mother or President Jefferson—Lewis wrote that he entertained "the most confident hope of succeeding."

By end of May 1805, just five days after Lewis penned his line about believing it "a good comfortable road until I am compelled to believe differently," he and the expedition were struggling to pull their pirogues upriver in frigid water that reached up to their armpits. And when they weren't in the water, they were dealing with slippery rocks, sharp rock fragments, or mud so thick the men couldn't wear their moccasins because it simply engulfed their footwear. Lewis described the labor as "incredibly painful and great." In other words, he and Clark now had ample evidence that the road was not going to be comfortable. Yet instead of dwelling on the difficulties, Lewis opted to spend a full three-fourths of his journal entry for that day documenting neither the difficulties nor the problems. He instead concentrated his attention on the "romantic appearance" of the White Cliffs that line the Missouri River in present-day Montana and the scenes of "visionary [enchantment]."

His reaction is characteristic of how both Lewis and Clark approached every difficult situation. They always emphasized the positive. They gave voice to the difficulties but never needlessly dwelled on them.

Two weeks later, Lewis and Clark were provided additional evidence that their road was not going to be a comfortable one when they encountered the Great Falls. They had been told to expect just one waterfall; instead, they found five. And what they had thought would be a short, half-day portage turned into a grueling month-long affair that pitted them and their men against the rugged terrain. Their feet were pierced by prickly pear cactus, and when the prickly pear was not a threat, the ground itself was. Weeks earlier, herds of buffalo had walked in the wet earth and left hoof marks that had now dried into sharp, pointed edges that punctured the men's moccasins. Over this forbidding terrain, the men had to carry canoes and equipment so heavy that they had to leverage every rock, branch, and piece of grass just to pull themselves forward. So tiring was the work that they literally fell asleep the moment the captains allowed them to rest.

By staying focused on the positive—and, in this case, the positive was that they were continuing to make progress—and by refusing to accept that the portage was anything more than a one-time challenge that would not be repeated, Lewis and Clark kept everyone moving on.

The Absence of Pessimism

A week later, with difficult portaging still remaining, Clark wrote "that we are now about to enter the most perilous and difficult part of our voyage, yet I see no one repining; all appear ready to meet those difficulties which wait us with resolution and becoming fortitude." The shift in attitude and tone is subtle, but it is evident that the "cheerfulness" has now been replaced with steely determination. What is especially telling is that no one is expressing any pessimism. I recall this passage because it reflects a realistic view of the situation and is the corollary to the principle of positive thinking, which is this: At some moments and in some situations, the most realistic form of optimism is simply the absence of pessimism.

Lewis and Clark, above all else, were authentic leaders. They understood that buoyant expressions of optimism at various times during the expedition would have rung hollow. So they did the next best thing, and that was not to give in to cynicism, negative thinking, or pessimism.

The Corps of Discovery eventually reached rock bottom during their courageous trip over the Bitterroot Mountains in September 1805. At times, they had to cut their own path through the wooded terrain, and at other times they got lost. They battled everything from snow, rain, and sleet to dangerous and rocky hills. Through it all, Lewis and Clark never once complained or despaired. Even when they were reduced to eating horse flesh and candles, the closest anyone came to complaining was when Private Joseph Whitehouse scribbled a three-word entry on September 2, 1805: "horrid bad going." But even he, five days later, after they had survived the Bitterroots, summed up the situation perfectly when he wrote that the men never once complained, "trusting to providence & the Conduct of our Officers in all our difficulties." In short, the men turned to Lewis and Clark during this most difficult period, and what they saw were two men who refused to become pessimistic. They, in turn, drew strength from their leaders' courage and optimism.

QUESTION LIMITS

As they came out of the Bitterroots and the Corps of Discovery saw flat land for the first time in weeks, they were thrilled. They then learned from the local Indians that the river they were on led to the Pacific. The future, it finally appeared, was looking brighter.

What they did not know was just how violent and difficult the rafting would be on this portion of the river. Many of the most dangerous sections of river have long since been submerged by the construction of dams, but at the turn of the nineteenth century, the Corps of Discovery faced a series of violent rapids (what would today be considered class-five rapids), and they did so in heavy, inflexible, wood canoes.

Having remained optimistic throughout the great portage and across the Bitterroots, Lewis and Clark took on the rapids without blinking. There are only two passages in the journals that even hint at the difficulty of this portion of the trip. On one occasion, Clark noted that the river actually looked a lot more violent once he was in it than it had appeared from the cliffs above when he first surveyed it. And a second time, he passively noted that a number of Indians, thinking the Corps of Discovery's trip down the rapids was suicidal, watched from the shore in the hope that they would be able to salvage some of the items that would float downriver after the canoes had inevitably capsized and the members perished.

Think about this scene for a moment. Here are natives—people who have lived on the river their whole lives (and their ancestors before them for generations)—waiting for a group of strangers to die because they were convinced that what they were about to undertake was impossible. Yet Lewis and Clark and the Corps of Discovery simply proceeded on, confident in their ability to overcome any and all obstacles. The story demonstrates how their optimism gave them the confidence to question limits. Just because the Indians said they didn't *believe* it could be done, didn't mean it *couldn't* be done.

The expedition had previously shown this same willingness to question limits in July 1805 when they were getting nervous about locating the Shoshone. Clark was extremely ill and suffering from chills and severe muscle pain, and the expedition was "now several [h]undred miles within the bosom of this wild and mountainous country, where game may rationally be expected shortly to become scarce and subsistence precarious." Worse still, the leaders had no idea how far the mountains continued. Yet, in the midst of this, Lewis wrote, "I still hope for the best." He based this comment on the fact "that if any Indians can subsist in the form of a nation in these mountains with the means they have of acquiring food we can also subsist."

It was a bold statement. Lewis was convinced of the Corps of Discovery's ability to survive based on nothing other than the fact that others had survived. That the Shoshone had horses and might have acquired and/or adopted skills over the centuries that were essential to mountainous living apparently never entered the mind of Meriwether Lewis. He simply believed that if others could do it, he and the Corps of Discovery could do it. Even later when Cameahwait, the leader of the Shoshone Indians, told him that the road over the mountain was a bad one and that his people had suffered excessively crossing the mountains, it did nothing to diminish Lewis's optimism. Again, he reasoned that if the Shoshone could do it, the Corps of Discovery could do it.

Focus on the Positive

One of the most remarkable passages of the entire expedition occurred on August 12, 1805. After discovering the headwaters of the Missouri River, Lewis climbed up what is today Lemhi Pass on the Montana-Idaho border and stood atop the Continental Divide. From this majestic perch, he looked to the west. Instead of finding a waterway meandering its way down the western slopes on a course that would ultimately flow to the Pacific Ocean, Lewis saw nothing but more mountain ranges.

He described the scene this way: "[We proceeded] on to the top of the dividing ridge from which I discovered immense ranges of high mountains still to the West of us with their tops partially covered with snow." The passage doesn't sound like much; but the reason it is so remarkable is because of what it *doesn't* say. Up until the very moment Lewis had actually climbed atop the Continental Divide and peered over, it had been accepted wisdom that there existed an all-water route connecting the Pacific and Atlantic oceans. Just as the Missouri River flowed east from the eastern slopes of the Rocky Mountains, it was assumed that a similar river flowed west to the Pacific. The continent, most experts of the day believed, could be joined by portaging a short distance between the two. Everyone from Christopher Columbus to President Jefferson believed that such a path existed. Even Meriwether Lewis accepted this bit of conventional wisdom as he walked up the eastern side of the Continental Divide. Imagine, then, his surprise when he saw not the actualization of a dream that spanned four centuries but the staggering new reality of more mountains— mountains as far as the eye could behold. John Logan Allen, the noted Lewis and Clark historian, wrote that it was at this very moment when the "geography of hope" gave way to "the geography of reality."[1]

But Meriwether Lewis, at a moment when it would have been easy—and perhaps natural—to have been not just surprised but downright depressed, instead simply noted the reality of the situation. It was what it was, and he and Captain Clark and the Corps of Discovery would just have to deal with the new reality.

It is at this point that Lewis and Clark demonstrated a real hallmark of leadership. After noting the "immense ranges of mountains," he immediately refocused the attention of the expedition to the one positive aspect of their newfound reality. He noted that they had now "tasted the water of the great Columbia River." This meant that, for the first time since the trip began, the Corps of Discovery was again headed downriver, where the current of the river was working in their favor. It wasn't a lot to hang one's hat on, but it was something, and Lewis latched on to it. The wind was "at their back," as it were, and he wasn't going to let anyone forget that fact.

By November 1805, after portaging the Great Falls, finding the Shoshone, crossing the Bitterroots, and navigating the wild Columbia River, the Corps of Discovery finally reached the coast and tasted the salty water of the Pacific Ocean. Lewis and Clark now had irrefutable proof that the journey was possible and the Corps of Discovery had experienced the tangible benefits of realistic optimism.

They still, however, had the daunting prospect of the return journey, in which they would have to work their way back up the fast-flowing Columbia River, recross the Bitterroots, and safely work their way back down the Missouri River and past the Teton Sioux again before they could claim complete success. And they had to do all of this with a supply list that was rapidly diminishing and had little prospect of being replenished. (There was a possibility that Lewis and Clark would meet up with a ship on the Pacific coast that could replenish their supplies, but the chance was remote and the captains certainly could not expect or count on such an event.)

All of these looming issues weighed on the minds of everyone from November 1805 to March 1806 as they camped at Fort Clatsop. The weather was cold and rainy the entire time, which only served to compound the situation. It would have been easy to despair, especially in light of the fact that the primary object of the mission—to find the most practicable water route to the Pacific—had not proven realistic. Furthermore, the liquor was all gone, food was increasingly difficult to find, and, at one point, the captains even ordered the men to stop engaging in sexual relations with the local Indian women. In short, there was little to be optimistic about except their eventual celebratory return to the United States, where they would be greeted by well-wishers and reunited with their family and friends. And it was upon this sentiment that Lewis and Clark appear to have focused their men's attention.

On January 1, 1806, with only water to drink and boiled elk to eat, Lewis leaped forward in his mind a year and anticipated January 1807. He noted in his journal that in exactly one year's time they would be "in the bosom of our friends . . . to participate in the mirth and hilarity of the day." And, in a testament to the power of positive thinking, that is precisely what Meriwether Lewis was doing on January 1, 1807, as he dined and celebrated with President Jefferson in the comfort of the White House.

Leading Into the Unknown

As many businesspeople will tell you, the most important factor in determining whether a venture will succeed—more important than any business plan, access to capital, or the advice of the best consultants—is the belief by the person undertaking the venture that it can be successfully accomplished. Henry Ford summed up this line of thinking when he said, "If you think you can do a thing or think you can't, you're right." It is all a matter of perspective. Lewis and Clark understood this, and, like many business leaders today, they were confronted with a seemingly endless number of challenges. Yet, by employing six traits of positive thinking, the captains were able to meet every challenge and overcome every obstacle in their path.

Start with the right mind-set. From the beginning, Lewis and Clark contemplated and visualized success. To both men, the world was full of possibilities and opportunities. They expected to enjoy the trip, they expected to make progress, and they expected to succeed. For the captains, the proverbial glass was always half full.

The visualization of future events is—and can be—a powerful motivator. In a landmark study that spanned thirty years and included numerous personal interviews, Dr. Martin Seligman, the author of *Learned Optimism*, discovered that one of the most significant predictors of success is optimistic expectations. He found that ability and motivation were often not enough in the absence of optimistic expectations, particularly in situations that required persistence to overcome adversity. Expectations of success or failure, he found, often become self-fulfilling prophecies.[2]

In his study, Seligman gave thousands of applicants for Met Life insurance salesperson positions his Attributional Style Questionnaire (ASQ). Among the many traits the questionnaire tested for was optimism. Met Life eventually hired over a thousand applicants based on their overall scores. Half of them, as it turned out, were rated as optimists and half pessimists. In the first year, Seligman found that the optimists were much less likely to quit and outsold the pessimists by 8 percent. In the second year, the optimists increased that percentage to 31 percent.

That same year, Met Life took the extraordinary step of hiring 129 additional salespersons who did not score well on the ASQ but scored exceptionally high on the optimism portion of the test.

What Seligman discovered was startling. Even though this small group lacked the other skills believed to be essential to success as a salesperson, the group outsold the pessimists by 21 percent in the first year and 57 percent the second year. Seligman repeated his studies with professional sports teams and even Senate and presidential candidates and found that pessimism consistently predicted failure.

Keep events in perspective. At the beginning of the trip, when Lewis and Clark lost one man to illness, another went missing for days, and a third deserted, they refused to view each event as anything but an isolated incident. By doing so, they were able to keep things in proportion and did not become overwhelmed by the situation. In business, employees are going to leave, the economy is going to slow, and competitors are going to develop new products. Sometimes all three will happen simultaneously. It is therefore important to remember that events are often unrelated and that they can be managed more easily if this simple fact is kept in mind.

Understand the difference between an obstacle and a barrier. The co-captains never viewed obstacles as barriers. In most instances, it was simply a matter of perspective. They held fast to two beliefs: If others before them had done it, they could also do it. And if others said it couldn't be done (e.g., rafting the Columbia River or crossing the Bitterroots), they possessed enough confidence in themselves to try it. An example of the first belief can be found in Michael Dell's decision to invest $1,000 of his own money and enter into direct competition with IBM and Hewlett-Packard in the computer manufacturing industry. His decision to sell custom-built personal computers is now the basis of a multibillion-dollar business. An example of the second belief can be found in Fred Smith's decision to start Federal Express. Smith faced daunting obstacles in starting an overnight express delivery system that could compete against the U.S. Postal Service and UPS, but because he could see the opportunity that lay beyond the barriers, he was able to succeed. Another example of the second belief can be found in Ted Turner's decision to start a twenty-four-hour news station. At the time, almost everyone said it couldn't be done—or that if it was attempted, it would not be successful. Turner decided to try, and today CNN is not just available twenty-four hours a day, it is available around the world.

Refuse to be pessimistic. On many occasions, Lewis and Clark had no reason to be optimistic, so they did the next best thing, which was to not become pessimistic. They refrained from complaining and feeling sorry for themselves. A good example is Meriwether Lewis's reaction upon first seeing the Great Falls. Instead of viewing it as a massive obstacle, Lewis focused instead on its natural beauty. The situation is not dissimilar to a business executive who, rather than worrying or complaining about a new competitor that has entered the market, instead views the competition as an opportunity to improve and reach an even higher level of performance.

Many of today's manufacturing businesses are facing a number of significant challenges from global competitors who enjoy cheaper labor costs and looser regulatory restrictions, and it is easy to despair. The optimistic business leader, however, will focus on those things that are still within his or her control. For instance, a manufacturer may still possess unique strengths in terms of quality or convenience, or have superior sales, servicing, or marketing capabilities. The executive must concentrate her resources on those strengths—and use them to build a competitive advantage.

Be realistic, but always keep a positive forward-focus. When Lewis peered over the Continental Divide and saw there was no short, easy passage, he instantly changed his focus to emphasize the fact that they were now, at least, on the "downhill" road. I believe the captains did the same thing after they reached the Pacific and had only the daunting prospect of the return journey to contemplate as they spent the winter at Fort Clatsop. To keep the Corps of Discovery from unnecessarily dwelling on this fact, the journals suggest that Lewis leaped forward in his mind to think about better times and visualize a successful return. The task for today's leader is to find similar sources or pockets of hope during tough times and focus people's attention on them. The practice not only diverts attention from the current negative situation, but provides positive motivation for the rest of the workforce to keep working toward that better future.

Optimism requires action. When Lewis and Clark saw the Rocky Mountains and the Bitterroots, they did not view the situation through rose-tinted glasses. They were realistic enough to understand that the obstacles before them would be difficult—but not impossible—to overcome. They embraced reality, they didn't hide from it. This approach allowed them to stay flexible and open to new ideas and new approaches. Moreover, on a daily basis they worked to improve their situation. This is an important point for today's business leaders because some people are simply "passive optimists" and assume things will get better as a result of external factors. Lewis and Clark were "active optimists" who never stopped working to improve their situation.

Proceed On!

Lewis and Clark might have easily succumbed to the insidious effects of pessimism. Other explorers had set out with the same goal of finding an all-water route to the Pacific and failed before they even reached the Mississippi. Few people would have criticized Lewis and Clark if they had also fallen short. Few would have blamed them if, upon reaching the Great Falls and discovering five waterfalls instead of one, they had opted to turn back, with the idea of trying again in the future with better equipment and more men. Who would have blamed them if they had simply retreated once they had peered over the Continental Divide and saw that a practical water route to the Pacific simply did not exist—for it was clear at that moment that one of their primary goals could not be accomplished. Yet they did not turn back. Lewis and Clark remained optimistic even when each day seemed to be more difficult than the day before.

They succeeded because they were confident from the beginning, focused on the positive, and viewed obstacles for what they were—challenges to be overcome, not insurmountable barriers. But, most of all, they were empowered by their belief that the next day would get better, and they actively worked to make it to the next day. Eventually, the days did get better—but only because Lewis and Clark believed that they would. Their success in overcoming the unknown became a self-fulfilling prophecy, and so can yours if you remain a realistic optimist.

CHAPTER NINE

RATIONAL RISK

The Principle of Aggressive Analysis

*Take calculated risks. That is quite different
from being rash.*
—General George Patton

By October 1805, the Corps of Discovery, after making their way 2,000 miles up the Missouri River, pushing over the Continental Divide, and crossing the Bitterroot Mountains, finally had the current of the river working in their favor. The only problem was that the western descent from the Rocky Mountains to the Pacific was much steeper than the rate at which the Missouri River had descended on the opposite side of the Rockies. This meant that the number of waterfalls and the severity of the rapids the Corps of Discovery would encounter would be greater and of a more violent nature than those which they had previously experienced.

On October 14, 1805, William Clark noted that the party had passed a number of rapids and eventually reached a very dangerous rapid that was three miles in length and very difficult to navigate. Even though the Corps of Discovery lost some valuable clothing, equipment, and supplies running the rapids, it is clear from Clark's writing that the Corps of Discovery never considered portaging the rapids. Winter was approaching, food was scarce, and the expedition was eager to reach the Pacific.

Ten days later, they were confronted with more rapids. After climbing to the top of a cliff with his most able waterman, Pierre Cruzatte, William Clark surveyed the situation. He matter-of-factly stated that the river compressed itself into a thin channel of about forty-five yards and the water was "swelling, boiling & whirling in every direction." He confidently wrote that "by good steering we could pass down safe." Again, the Corps of Discovery safely shot the rapids.

The following day Lewis and Clark were confronted with even more rapids. In spite of their earlier success, however, the risk was just too great and they decided to "[m]ake a portage of our most valuable articles" and assigned the nonswimmers to walk the route and carry the supplies. (Still, the canoes were too heavy to portage and some of the men had to raft the river.)

How they dealt with these different rapids is revealing. The co-commanders were at times willing to risk the entire expedition to the perils of the wild river, but at other times they opted for a slower, more cautious approach. In many ways their flexibility, as well as their ability to weigh the costs and benefits of the respective rapids, was the epitome of their entire journey. In short, they were fearless but never reckless. This sentiment captures the ninth leadership principle of Lewis and Clark, rational risk: the principle of aggressive analysis.

Prioritizing Goals

To lead is to make decisions. Over the course of the twenty-eight-month expedition, Lewis and Clark made countless decisions. Most were minor, but many were very significant. Lewis and Clark's decisions about personnel were reviewed in Chapter Four and clearly rank as the most important decisions they made. However, eleven other decisions shed valuable insight into the co-leaders' decision-making process and help demonstrate how they analyzed situations, weighed options, and came to make some of their more momentous decisions.

PRUDENT PRIORITIZATION

Once the trip was under way, the first decision of note was their decision to leave Pierre Dorion, a skilled Sioux interpreter, behind. In August 1804, Lewis and Clark were well aware that the powerful Teton Sioux still lay ahead and that the tribe posed a far greater threat to the expedition than any tribe they had yet encountered. (The Teton Sioux were the strongest tribe, in both military and economic terms, on the Northern Plains. This strength was based in large measure on their positive trade relations with British and French traders. The Americans were therefore viewed warily by the Sioux, but with hope by the Arikara and Yankton, who felt they could break the Sioux's lock on power.) But rather than retain the services of Dorion, Lewis and Clark opted to leave him behind with the Yankton Sioux to help negotiate a peace treaty between the Yankton and the Arikara Indians. The decision indicates that the captains placed a high priority on the goal of establishing peace, and that this goal transcended any concern they had about being able to effectively communicate with the Teton Sioux. It also suggests that the captains did not overanticipate problems. Lewis and Clark knew that Dorion could definitely help the Yankton negotiate a peace. They therefore chose to employ his services dealing with this known problem, rather than keeping him in reserve for a future problem that might never materialize.

Near the end of their expedition, Lewis and Clark again demonstrated their ability to prioritize when they made the important—and potentially costly—decision to split up and explore new areas separately. In spite of their longing to return to civilization and be reunited with their families and loved ones, they divided up the expedition into five smaller parties. The wisdom of this decision, made in the middle of hostile territory was—and still is—questionable. Yet, it was neither a reckless nor a foolish decision. Meriwether Lewis traveled north up the Marias for a very important reason: He wanted to determine the northernmost point of the river in the hope he would find that a portion of the river was located above the forty-ninth parallel. Such a discovery, under the terms of an earlier treaty, would secure additional territory for the United States. As it turned out, Lewis's side trip was a failure. In spite of waiting two full days in an attempt to determine accurately how far north he was, Lewis was forced to return without any useful information because the clouds never cleared long enough to allow him to fix his location by use of his sextant. And the trip was counterproductive because it was during this excursion that Lewis had his deadly encounter with the Blackfeet Indians and thus spoiled any realistic chance that the United States would be able to establish peaceful relations with the powerful Blackfeet nation.

Because of these events, the decision has been widely criticized by historians and others. Yet had Lewis been successful in either securing more land for the United States or accomplishing his diplomatic efforts, it is probable that history would have applauded his decision. It is only fair, then, that the decision be viewed in the context of the information that was known beforehand to Meriwether Lewis. In this light, the decision, while risky, was conceived with good intentions and had a fair probability of success. It is again revealing that neither Lewis nor Clark opted against conducting the side trip out of fear that something bad *might* happen.

Limiting Your Downside

Lewis and Clark's decision at the Marias, which was recounted extensively in Chapter Six, is worth reviewing from the perspective of the captains' ability to manage risk. After they had surveyed the situation, sent separate parties up each river, and traveled far up the rivers themselves, Lewis and Clark came to the correct conclusion that the southern fork of the river represented the true Missouri. In so doing, however, they also acted to limit their downside by sending Meriwether Lewis up ahead with a small advance party to scout the Great Falls. It was Lewis's responsibility to turn around if it became evident that their decision was wrong. The captains did not have to exercise this option, but it is still telling that they hedged against an incorrect decision.

In August 1805, the two leaders again demonstrated similar thinking when they opted to send William Clark ahead to investigate whether the Salmon River was unnavigable, as the Shoshone had suggested. Having been misinformed about the existence of the Marias River, as well as the length of the portage at the Great Falls, Lewis and Clark now viewed Indian information with a jaundiced eye. Still, they had received enough good information that they weren't going to dismiss it out of hand.

Clark confirmed the Shoshone information in a matter of days and saved the expedition precious time by ruling out the Salmon River as a viable option.

These two decisions are instructive because Lewis and Clark were clearly willing to make aggressive decisions, but they rarely did so without hedging against the possibility that they might be incorrect. Nor did they let their confidence in themselves blind them to the possibility that they might be wrong.

A variation of this theme was employed in the middle of their forced march over the Bitterroot Mountains (also recounted in detail in Chapter Six). Facing cold, miserable conditions and nearing starvation, Lewis and Clark conferred and decided to send Clark ahead in search of food and a positive indication that the difficult mountain range was giving way to flatter land. On both accounts, Clark was successful. And although he didn't send a lot of food back to the remainder of the expedition, what little he did send, along with the news that they were near the end, was enough to lift the crew's morale at what would be its lowest point during the entire expedition. The decision to send Clark ahead essentially stemmed the slide and helped reinforce the Corps of Discovery's resolve when it was most in danger of dissipating.

Adaptability

On July 4, 1805, having recently completed their portage around the Great Falls and having just used up the last of their whiskey rations, Lewis wrote that "not having seen the [Shoshone] or knowing in fact whether to calculate on their friendship or hostility . . . we have conceived our party sufficiently small and therefore have concluded not to dispatch a canoe with a part of our men to St. Louis as we had intended early in the spring." From the passage, it is evident that Lewis and Clark had intended at one point to send a second crew back to St. Louis with their latest findings. For two reasons, they decided otherwise. First, the captains were concerned that the Shoshone might be hostile, so they reasoned that they would need as many men as possible to maximize their fighting strength. Second, they concluded that to send some men back at this point might so discourage those who remained that it could seriously impede the party's ability to move forward.

This decision not only demonstrates Lewis and Clark's skill in assimilating different information, but offers proof that they remained adaptable and confident enough in themselves to change their minds when confronted with new realities. In this instance, Lewis and Clark reasoned that the benefits of sending new information back to President Jefferson did not outweigh the risks associated with reducing the party and lowering morale.

Bias in Favor of Forward Movement

In August 1805, Cameahwait, the Shoshone chieftain, warned Lewis and Clark that a trek across the Bitterroots was next to impossible and that even if they did survive, food on the other side was so scarce that the Corps of Discovery would be exposed to extreme hardship. Cameahwait let it be known that he had this information because some of his own people had themselves made the difficult trip and had reported back about the tribes living on the other side. Lewis chose to focus his attention not on Cameahwait's assessment of the difficulty of the journey, but rather on the fact that they had successfully crossed. In his journal, Lewis put it this way: "I felt perfectly satisfied, that if the Indians could pass these mountains . . . that we could also pass them." Furthermore, he noted "that if nations on this river below the mountains were as numerous as they were stated to be that they must have some means of subsistence which it would be equally in our power to procure in the same country." The passage not only captures Lewis's wonderful confidence in himself and the Corps of Discovery, but also reflects his bias for forward movement. Lewis and Clark understood the risks but opted to move ahead anyway. The fact that some Shoshone had crossed the mountains, coupled with the knowledge that people were surviving on the other side of the mountains, provided the captains everything they needed to know about their prospects for survival: *If others could do it, they could do it.*

A second instance of Lewis and Clark's bias toward forward movement occurred in early April 1806, just as they were setting out from Fort Clatsop on their return trip to St. Louis. The Indians had informed the two co-commanders that food was scarce in the land west of the Bitterroots and that the annual salmon run (which would have provided the Corps of Discovery with the necessary food stock to survive) would not occur for at least another month. The choice was either wait for an ample supply of food or press on. Lewis quickly concluded that to wait "would detain us so large a portion of the season that it is probable we should not reach the United States before the ice would close the Missouri; or at all events would hazard our horses which we left in charge of the Chopunnish [Nez Percé] who informed us that they intended passing the rocky mountains . . . bout the beginning of May."

In other words, Lewis and Clark had to risk either spending another year in the wilderness or starvation. Lewis and Clark chose the latter. Their decision-making process once again demonstrated that when forced to select between two difficult options, they opted for the one that kept them moving forward. The decision also reinforces the early theme that Lewis and Clark were never paralyzed by the fear of what might occur. They were told that food *might* be scarce—but they knew *for certain* that if they didn't meet up with the Nez Percé, they would not be reunited with their horses.

"Patience, Patience"

Lewis and Clark were not, however, recklessly aggressive. When the captains were presented with compelling information or confronted with staggering odds, they were willing to exercise patience. For instance, after the Corps of Discovery had decided to push up the Columbia River with little food, their decision paid off when they arrived at Camp Chopunnish and reconnected with the Nez Percé. Within days, Lewis noted that the river was rapidly rising and correctly attributed it to the melting snows in the Bitterroots or, in his own words, "that icy barrier which separates me from my friends and Country." Having risked much to get to this point, the entire expedition was very anxious to proceed. Yet, Lewis and Clark understood that more snow had to melt. Lewis concluded his journal entry for that day with the words "patience, patience."

For the better part of a month, the Corps of Discovery waited for the snows to melt. The strength of character Lewis and Clark displayed during this time was immense. At this point in the expedition, they had been away from home for two years. Moreover, they were subsisting on a diet of horsemeat and roots, though they knew that on the other side of the mountains lay a bounty of buffalo and other game. To make matters even worse, the spring sun—which was perfect for traveling—warmed the valley and made the men even more restless to get moving. Still, Lewis and Clark waited.

Their willingness to wait so long demonstrated that Lewis and Clark would not be rushed into a hasty decision. Finally, on June 10, 1806, against the advice of the local Indians, the captains reasoned that the mountains were passable and ordered the Corps of Discovery to move out and reconquer the Bitterroots.

Reverse Course

As it turned out, they were not quite patient enough in their desire to recross the Bitterroots. Four days into the journey, Lewis's journal entry read as though he was trying to convince himself of the necessity of departing before the Indians said it would be safe. He complained of already being detained five weeks and noted that it was "a serious loss of time at this delightful season for traveling." He added that "every body seems anxious to be in motion, convinced that we have not now any time to delay if the calculation is to reach the United States this season." He concluded his entry for the day in his characteristic upbeat, optimistic fashion: "I am determined to accomplish if within the compass of human power."

His optimism seemed to pay off, for over the next few days the party encountered signs of spring everywhere. There were violets, columbines, and bluebells in bloom and their sweet scent hung in the air. Then, on June 17, they encountered snow "twelve to fifteen feet deep." Lewis and Clark conferred and reviewed the facts. They knew they were at least five days away from a reliable source of food and water for their horses. They also understood that if they didn't reach the location within that time, not only would their horses be in jeopardy but so would all of the equipment the horses were carrying.

With these facts in mind, Lewis and Clark reached one of their most crucial decisions of the entire expedition. For the only time in the entire journey, they ordered a retrograde march. The reality of the situation outweighed their penchant for moving forward.

That evening, with rain falling on them as if to add to their misery, they returned to camp and waited an additional seven days for the snows to melt. The difficulty they encountered in their attempt to recross the mountains also caused Lewis and Clark to reverse their decision not to hire local guides. Portions of their trip back across the Bitterroots had been so dangerous that they came to realize that their limited knowledge of the area was a threat to their own safety. Lewis and Clark therefore agreed to pay the extraordinary sum of two guns to hire a trio of local Indians to guide them back over the range. On June 24, they set out again. Less than a week later, on June 30, Clark reported that they descended the mountain to Traveler's Rest, "leaving those tremendious mountains behind us."

The decision to reverse course had been a difficult one from a psychological perspective, and the decision to hire local guides had been costly in terms of having to give up two guns, but both proved to be prudent. As a consequence, no one got hurt on the trip, and the Corps of Discovery made excellent time recrossing the Bitterroots. Whereas the first trip had taken eleven days, the return trip, utilizing the skill and knowledge of the local Indians, took only six.

By honestly assessing the situation and refusing to be reckless, Lewis and Clark demonstrated the sound judgment that was one of their most consistent characteristics and an integral component of their success.

Leading Into the Unknown

Managing risk will always be one of the most important functions of any leader. Lewis and Clark's experiences, as well as their approach to risk, hold a number of tangible lessons for today's business executive. Among these are:

Deal with known problems first. Lewis and Clark refused to be paralyzed by the mere possibility of future problems. When confronted with a choice between dealing with a known problem and keeping something in reserve to handle a potential future problem, they chose to deal with the here and now. Neither Lewis nor Clark ever discussed in their journals their decision-making process, and it is difficult to draw direct parallels with today's business environment, but one modern business tool the captains may have well understood would be the prioritization matrix. This quantitative tool allows various scenarios to be ranked according to importance, frequency, and feasibility. It is used to help businesses better understand and weigh their options. The one area where the captains might have differed with it is that they clearly discounted the likelihood of negative outcomes occurring in the future. While this is neither an inherently positive nor a negative characteristic, it is telling. According to a *Harvard Business Review* article, companies that had a more optimistic view of the future—even if that optimism was not based on sound analysis—were more likely to aggressively approach the future.[1]

Favor forward movement. In many instances, the risks associated with moving forward are not significantly different from those associated with staying put. In these situations, Lewis and Clark always opted for the decision that would keep the Corps of Discovery moving forward.

The business world is littered with examples of companies and executives with a bias in favor of forward movement. In spite of an uncertain future environment, many companies will take a calculated risk and move ahead. For instance, the Fidelity Fund, the precursor to Fidelity Investments, the world's largest mutual fund company, was started in 1930, at the height of the Great Depression. In 1991, in the middle of a recession, Intel Corp. invested $5 billion in factories to manufacture the Pentium chip. And, more recently, JetBlue Airways, in the wake of the 2001 terrorist attacks, doubled its fleet and was one of only two airlines to make a profit in 2002.[2]

Limit your downside. Lewis and Clark were aggressive leaders, but they were not reckless. In many instances, the captains hedged against failure by sending one of the co-commanders ahead in the event that they were wrong. In the business world, there are scores of savvy executives who have successfully hedged their bets. For instance, in the late 1990s, after almost missing out on the opportunity presented by the Internet, Microsoft Corp. paid $600 million for a small stake in Nextel Communications and another $5 billion for a similar share of AT&T Corp. to make sure it didn't miss out on the wireless market. Scores of other companies—from medical device makers and pharmaceutical companies to semiconductor and data storage companies—make sizable investments in promising start-ups on the chance that they might produce a major commercial product. These investments ensure that if they have chosen the "wrong fork in the river" (to use the analogy of Lewis and Clark at the Marias), they at least have a strategy for quickly minimizing their downside.

Demonstrate patience. Whether it meant waiting forty extra days to get the keelboat, patiently biding their time to recross the Bitterroots, or even delaying the start of their trip by one month (which they did in the spring of 1804), Lewis and Clark refused to be rushed into hasty or bad decisions. This is a particularly appropriate lesson for businesses that have only one chance to make a favorable impression in the marketplace or, alternatively, have a product that can ill afford to be anything but 100 percent effective. Rushing to market with either an inferior or a flawed product can be counterproductive. As Lewis and Clark demonstrated when they entered the Bitterroots too early, such hasty decisions can end up costing a lot more than originally planned and, if one is not careful, can even prove fatal.

Reverse course when appropriate. Lewis and Clark had an amazing string of successes throughout their entire trip. Their confidence in themselves and their men was extraordinary. Yet when confronted with a return trip over the Bitterroots that was simply too risky, the captains did not hesitate to order a retrograde march. They did not let their previous successes blind them to real dangers.

In many ways, Lewis and Clark's decision was analogous to The Coca-Cola Company's infamous New Coke decision. For years, Coca-Cola had been the dominant cola beverage, controlling upwards of 24 percent of the market share. In the early 1980s, however, PepsiCo introduced the Pepsi Challenge, a clever advertising campaign encouraging people to take a blind taste test. The ads were clearly hitting their mark. Almost overnight, Pepsi's market share jumped 8 percent. Worse for Coca-Cola, independent taste tests confirmed the findings of the Pepsi Challenge. The executives at Coca-Cola quickly ordered their researchers to find a better formula and directed their marketing team to determine if the company could effectively introduce a new product. Before long, a new formula, dubbed "New Coke," was developed that could beat Pepsi at its own game.

Coca-Cola launched the product in spite of some internal analysis that suggested that abandoning the "Original Coke" formula was not a wise strategy. Initially, public reaction to the new product was muted. But soon the "Old Coke" loyalists started speaking out and a previously apathetic public, fueled by media reports, began to voice their unhappiness with the new product. The situation became untenable and then-CEO Roberto Goizueta ordered a "retrograde march" and New Coke was killed.

This familiar story is often offered as an example of a bad business decision, but there are some important aspects of the New Coke story that don't often get retold. Goizueta, after taking the reins of the company in the early 1980s, successfully introduced Diet Coke. At the time, the decision was not universally hailed, but it clearly demonstrated Goizueta's penchant for exploring new ideas and taking calculated risks. And by 1985, it was clear that the decision to move forward with Diet Coke was extremely successful.

I recount this fact because Goizueta, like Lewis and Clark, had a bias in favor of action. Moreover, like the captains, he was operating from a history of success. (He had also successfully introduced Cherry Coke.) Yet it is telling that when confronted with the facts about New Coke, Goizueta did not rest on his past successes and try to "stay the course"; instead, he wisely reversed course. Similarly, like Lewis and Clark, Goizueta did not succumb to the hubris that just because his previous decisions had been successful, he could assume all of his subsequent decisions would also be correct.

Proceed On!

In late July 1806, there was a telling moment in the Lewis and Clark expedition. Meriwether Lewis had spotted a number of horses and rightly surmised that they belonged to the Blackfeet Indians. Lewis had hoped to avoid "an interview" with this powerful tribe, whom the Nez Percé had warned would "cut us off." Through his telescope he saw that the Blackfeet had spotted one of his men, George Droulliard. He was at a great enough distance that he and the other two members of his party could have fled. Lewis quickly considered and discarded the idea. To have fled would have sacrificed Droulliard to the Blackfeet. Instead, Lewis briskly and confidently approached the Blackfeet with an open hand. He did this in part to save Droulliard. It was, however, also a calculated risk designed to achieve a diplomatic victory. If the Blackfeet accepted his peaceful overture, Lewis surmised, he could use it as an opportunity to establish peaceful relations with this powerful tribe. Setting aside his fear, he moved forward and seized the moment. As history has recorded, however, Lewis failed in his effort to establish diplomatic relations.

I conclude with this rare failure because it serves as a reminder that in the end, risk is just that—risk. The best analysis in the world cannot always prevent every failure, but through reasoned and applied analysis, the odds of success can be greatly increased. And as Lewis and Clark demonstrated, you do not necessarily have to be perfect to succeed—you do, however, need to keep moving forward.

CHAPTER TEN

CULTIVATING A CORPS OF DISCOVERY
The Principle of Developing Team Spirit

*Morale is a state of mind. It is steadfastness
and courage and hope. It is confidence and
zeal and loyalty. It is élan, esprit de corps,
and determination.*

—General George Marshall

In his seminal work *Lewis and Clark Among the Indians,* James
Ronda wrote about Lewis and Clark's persevering through
patience, skill, and courage until "the Corps of Discovery found
its own soul." Ronda wasn't trying to make some deep philosophical point, and he didn't bring up the issue again in his book,
but it does raise an intriguing question. When did the Corps of
Discovery discover its soul? The short, honest answer is that we
will never know. I doubt that any member of the Corps of
Discovery, or even Lewis or Clark for that matter, could answer
the question with any specificity.

This has not stopped me from pondering the question, and as I researched this book, I came to believe that there was no one single place where it discovered its soul, nor was there a single event from which the discovery stemmed. Rather, its soul—by which I mean the spirit of teamwork and which I will henceforth refer to as spirit—was developed over time and through a series of events. The captains had everything to do with developing this spirit, and it is the basis for the tenth and final leadership principle of Lewis and Clark, cultivating a Corps of Discovery: the principle of developing team spirit.

Although there was no one single event that created the Corps of Discovery's spirit, I do believe there was a single moment when we know for certain that that spirit was present. But before I describe this event, it is first necessary to provide some background.

Founded on Trust

The expedition team didn't officially become the Corps of Discovery until after they departed from Fort Mandan and Lewis and Clark dispatched the return party back down the Missouri in April 1805. It was at this point that the thirty-three remaining members of the expedition became the "permanent party." This was the group that ventured to the Pacific Ocean and back.

After leaving Fort Mandan, the Corps of Discovery for the first time was truly exploring unknown territory. No American of European descent had ever walked the ground, and it was during this six-month stretch of the journey that they found their spirit.

The captains must have intuitively sensed that this portion of the expedition was going to be unique and that they would need to rely more on each other. It is why they abandoned their old style of military discipline and adopted a kinder, gentler, and more positive approach to management after leaving Fort Mandan (as documented in Chapter Five).

The first indication that the Corps of Discovery was beginning to develop a spirit occurred in mid-May 1805. The expedition members had already had a few run-ins with grizzly bears by this time, and their respect for the powerful creatures had increased immensely. As a result, they now often went out in teams. On May 14, a group of six men spotted a grizzly and orchestrated a coordinated attack. Four men fired their rounds into the bear—to little effect. The now-angry bear gave chase, and the two men who had been held in reserve for just such a contingency fired their rifles. Their bullets only temporarily halted the bear's progress, and it continued its pursuit. Two of the party dropped their guns and sprinted for the river in a desperate attempt to evade the bear, which was about to catch them, when an unidentified member of the party who had reloaded his rifle during the commotion took aim and coolly plugged the bear in the head, killing it.

The incident was just the first of many such incidents that made the expedition members realize how truly dependent they were on each other in this new territory, and it is one of the earliest examples of how they were coming together as a team and learning to trust one another.

A similar incident occurred a few days later when a sudden gust of wind nearly capsized the main pirogue. Meriwether Lewis and William Clark looked on in horror from the riverbank as water poured into the severely listing vessel. Lewis was so mortified that he contemplated jumping in the frigid, fast-moving waters of the Missouri and swimming to the craft until he realized that the idea was suicide. To his surprise, however, Pierre Cruzatte had enough presence of mind to order Charbonneau to maintain the helm while Sacagawea valiantly scrambled to retrieve items that were floating away or were in danger of sinking. Once again the team had saved the day. This time, however, it was Lewis and Clark who had learned that they could begin trusting their team to perform in difficult situations.

The third incident occurred less than a week afterward, when they reached the fork in the Marias River. Every person, save Lewis and Clark, believed the north fork was the true Missouri River. The captains overruled them and ordered the party down the south fork. In spite of this disagreement, the team felt Lewis and Clark had at least listened to their arguments, and they all "cheerfully" went along with the decision. A few days later, when the team heard the roaring waterfalls, the tables had now been reversed, and it was the Corps of Discovery who were learning to trust Lewis and Clark.

The Corps of Discovery's spirit really began to grow during their brutal eighteen-mile portage around the Great Falls. This was the group's first real challenge, and the work was so strenuous that when the captains allowed the men a break, some of them instantly fell asleep. The portage, which they had to do four times in order to transport all their equipment, demonstrated the power of teamwork and confirmed their ability to continue to move forward under even the most trying of circumstances.

The journals do not recount the following story in any detail, but there is a wonderful scene that occurred in the middle of the excruciating portage. In an effort to ease their immense burden, the team fashioned together a wagon to carry many of their items and then hoisted a sail upon it. By all accounts the makeshift contraption worked, and Lewis in his journal simply stated, "[T]his is Saleing on Dry land in every Sence of the word." It is a shame the story isn't elaborated on in the journals because if it were, it is my belief we might have learned that Patrick Gass, the carpenter, helped build the wagon; John Shields, the blacksmith, assisted in forging parts together; Sacagawea mended the oilcloth that was used as the sail; and it may have been Pierre Cruzatte, the half-French, half-Omaha Indian boatman who had grown up on the river who suggested that they try "dry sailing." In short, the scene would have been a glowing testament to the group's coming together as a team.

Regardless of whether that is how the scene came together, it was clear by this stage that everyone had begun to understand just how valuable every member of the expedition was to the overall success of the mission.

Their trust and belief in one another was forever forged during their trip across the Bitterroot Mountains. It has been called "one of the great forced marches in history."[1] Facing near starvation, dangerous conditions, and bone-chilling weather, the entire group refused to quit until they triumphed. As they emerged from the mountains and saw the prairie to the west, the spirit of the Corps of Discovery was undeniable.

This spirit was then honed and polished once they entered the final leg of their trip to the Pacific and rafted down the dangerous rapids of the Columbia River, which they almost laughed off as obstacles. With little hesitation, even party members who couldn't swim took the rapids head-on. As a team, they had come to believe they were capable of almost anything—and they were right.

All of these experiences—from the western edge of today's North Dakota to the Pacific Coast—were, however, leading up to one singular moment, and that was the historic vote at Chinook Point. It was here that every member of the expedition—including York and Sacagawea—was given the right to vote on the important issue of where they wanted to spend the winter.

Lewis and Clark could have just selected a location and ordered the Corps of Discovery to establish camp at that point. But they didn't. What they did was unprecedented in the annals of military history. They let everyone have an equal say in the decision.

It was at this unique moment that I believe one can say that the Corps of Discovery possessed a fully functioning spirit. Given everything they had been through up to that point, and given how much they had come to rely on one another, it seems only appropriate that each and every member be given an equal voice. That it occurred on the shores of the Pacific, after they had just conquered the unknown, isn't a coincidence. By this time, the Corps of Discovery had found that the journey of discovery was not only an exploration of physical spaces but an exploration—and discovery—of themselves and each other.

A Team from the Beginning

How they got to this point is not a mystery. Long before Lewis and Clark even left on their journey, they were laying the foundation and creating an atmosphere conducive to team building. From the beginning, the members of the Corps of Discovery knew that the expedition they were undertaking was special. Lewis and Clark articulated the vision and explained the goals to every member. They were to find the most navigable route to the Pacific, document scientific discoveries for the enlightened world, and make the path safe for their fellow countrymen.

Next, Lewis and Clark selected the team entirely on merit. Only men who would pull their own weight—and then some— were chosen. Instantly, the expedition members experienced the feeling of being part of an elite group. Lewis and Clark's own unique power-sharing arrangement also signaled that ego and glory were secondary to the success of the mission.

And lastly, the captains' willingness to do whatever was necessary—from acquiring the best equipment to increasing the size of the party to delaying the departure of the expedition an entire month in order to obtain extra items—sent the message that they were fully committed to success. If experts, such as George Droulliard (an interpreter and hunter), were needed, they were hired. If important rules (like the one requiring all men to be young and single) required exceptions, they were granted (as in the case of the married John Shields).

Lewis and Clark made their first real, tangible team-building decision immediately upon setting out on their journey from Camp Dubois in May 1804, when they decided to place all the members of what would eventually become the permanent party in the main keelboat. Those individuals who would return from Fort Mandan to St. Louis (called "the return party") were placed in a separate boat, while the French boatmen who were hired only to help navigate the first leg of the expedition up the Missouri were placed in another. The decision proved wise because it immediately gave the permanent party an opportunity to work closely together. Their struggle to push, pull, row, and sail the boat up against the mighty current of the Missouri can be thought of as an early "bonding" experience.

The second strategic team-building decision occurred in August 1804 after the death of Sergeant Charles Floyd. For reasons never elaborated on in their journals, Lewis and Clark polled their men on whom they wanted to replace Floyd as sergeant. Patrick Gass received nineteen votes and William Bratton eleven.

Lewis and Clark did not have to allow the election. In fact, at the time (and ever since), military commanders have had the authority to promote whomever they want when conditions war- rant it. The election of a sergeant in the U.S. Army was—and remains—without precedent. Their decision is one of the earliest and most vivid examples of the captains' respect for—and trust in—the Corps of Discovery. With this decision, they were essen- tially saying, "This is *our* Journey of Discovery."

Authentic Leadership

Some have speculated that Lewis and Clark allowed the election to stand only because they favored Gass. They believe that if one of the other men had won, Lewis and Clark would still have appointed Gass. I disagree with the theory because the captains, above all else, were authentic. Webster's dictionary defines *authentic* as being "true to one's own personality, spirit, or charac- ter," and I believe it was their authenticity that would have pre- vented them from authorizing an election and then nullifying its results. For Lewis and Clark, their word was their bond. And it was this authentic leadership that lay at the heart of Lewis and Clark's ability to cultivate the Corps of Discovery and create a team that was motivated, disciplined, and capable of meeting every challenge and overcoming every obstacle.

How did Lewis and Clark do it? There was no one thing. Rather, it was a combination of a number of different qualities. It began with the time-tested leadership trait of never asking those under you to do anything that you are unwilling to do yourself. As outlined in Chapter Six, at every critical moment, either Captain Lewis or Captain Clark was present and offered real leadership. Lewis and Clark also shared in the small daily sacrifices. They did not hesitate to carry supplies, cook for their men, or get out and push or pull the keelboat if that was what was required. Their willingness to partake in "the dangers and fatigues" also signaled that they respected their men. It demonstrated that they fully understood the burdens and difficulties they were assigning their team on a daily basis.

Lewis and Clark's respect for their men manifested itself in other ways, too. For instance, at the Marias, although the captains did not agree with the men's analysis of which river was the true Missouri, it is clear from their journals that either they solicited the men's opinions or, alternatively, the enlisted men felt comfortable enough with Lewis and Clark to voice their disagreement. Either way, it was clear that Lewis and Clark listened to their concerns. And in a further sign of respect, the captains demonstrated that they thought highly enough of the others' opinions that they hedged against the possibility of an incorrect decision by sending Lewis ahead. In essence, they were saying to the enlisted men, "You may be right."

At another point in the journey, William Bratton fell extremely ill, and in spite of all the treatments Lewis and Clark prescribed, nothing was working. John Shields then suggested that Bratton be sweated. The captains listened, and the treatment worked. While it is not the most poignant example, I retell the story to demonstrate that Lewis and Clark showed their respect in small as well as large ways.

The Intangibles

Because Lewis and Clark practiced what Tom Peters would call "management by walking around," meaning that they were walking and talking with their team members on a daily basis, not only were the captains approachable, but they were also able to keep their finger on the pulse of their team, so as to settle any problems and prevent rumors from spreading before they could have a negative impact on morale. The remarkable absence of major mistakes, fights, and rumors over the course of the long expedition is a testament to the captains' remarkable skills in this area.

But Lewis and Clark's character went beyond their dealings with the men. The captains always showed unfailing respect for each other, and they treated the native Indians with similar courtesy and respect. In this sense, Lewis and Clark led by example and set the tone for the whole journey.

Lewis and Clark's curiosity, resourcefulness, and openness to new ideas also went a long way toward fostering the spirit of the Corps of Discovery. The men could not help but appreciate the almost childlike curiosity of the captains as well as their inquisitive nature. Nor could they fail to notice the benefits that these characteristics produced. From the discovery of new plants and animals to a better understanding of the road ahead, the captains, by their actions, helped instill a sense of curiosity and resourcefulness in the Corps of Discovery.

From building better canoes to gelding their horses to finding resourceful solutions to problems—such as the time they used the old burned-out iron stove to fashion arrow tips, which they then traded for corn during the long, cold winter at Fort Mandan—Lewis and Clark were always thinking ahead, and they never hesitated to adopt a new method if it proved more effective. This willingness to learn and try new things was passed on to the Corps of Discovery and helped cultivate these same characteristics in their team.

Lewis and Clark also appear to have adopted an attitude of "not sweating the small stuff." This is not to say that they didn't pay attention to details. As outlined in Chapter Three, their willingness to pack and repack the keelboat, their emphasis on purchasing more blue beads than white beads, and Clark's insistence on walking an additional seven miles at the end of a long day to ensure that they didn't alert any Indians to their presence proved they were willing to go the extra mile and do the small things essential for success. But when avoidable mistakes were made, Lewis and Clark did not so much use them as an opportunity to punish as they did view them as learning experiences.

One explanation may have been that the captains made a good number of mistakes themselves. For instance, when Lewis went up the north fork (now known to be the Marias), he and his small party spent the better part of an afternoon building a raft to float back down the river. After a few hours of work, the task proved impractical. Rather than force the issue, Lewis swallowed his pride and simply abandoned the project and ordered his men to resume their hike back downriver. He did not second-guess himself. He just moved forward with a new, albeit slower, plan.

The same thinking was evident after Lewis and the Corps of Discovery had spent the better part of two weeks constructing the iron-frame boat. Lewis had a lot of pride riding on the project. He had hauled the frame 2,000 miles upriver and delayed the expedition during the height of the traveling season in order to build it. When it failed, due to a lack of pine tar to adhere the animal skins to the frame, he didn't push the matter; again, he just proceeded on. By being open about his mistakes, Lewis proved he was human, too, and this, in turn, wittingly or unwittingly, further helped to cultivate team spirit.

On a deeper level, however, I suspect Lewis and Clark recognized that focusing on mistakes was counterproductive to the long-term success of their mission. They understood that the spirit of exploration was one of moving forward, not dwelling on the past. The best example of Lewis and Clark's forgiving a mistake occurred after Pierre Cruzatte, near the end of the expedition, confused Lewis's buckskin coat for an elk and shot Lewis. By almost every imaginable standard, Lewis had a right to be furious with Cruzatte. After all, he had almost killed him. Both captains, however, scarcely mentioned the issue again. The reason, I submit, is because they understood that they were still in hostile territory. To punish Cruzatte might cause him, in the future, to hesitate in a situation where even the slightest hesitation could literally mean the difference between life and death. By using mistakes as learning opportunities rather than opportunities to punish, the captain ensured that the Corps of Discovery did not develop a rigid inflexibility—where the fear of doing something wrong triumphed over a willingness to act. This attitude went a long way toward cultivating the Corps of Discovery's innovative and aggressive spirit.

Genuine Concern

At the core of Lewis and Clark's authenticity was the timeless trait of genuine concern for their team. From their earliest preparations, Lewis and Clark worked to ensure that they were well supplied with the necessities for their survival. They had shirts, socks, coats, and, of course, weapons. This might seem an obvious thing, but in the military of the early nineteenth century, such necessities were not always guaranteed. The captains also, with a few exceptions, ensured that all the members of the party had food on a daily basis. This meant feeding thirty-three people (sometimes as many as fifty people early on in the expedition) three meals a day—for two and a half years. This works out to well over 100,000 separate meals. It was no small feat, especially considering that they consumed upwards of nine pounds of meat a day![2]

Lewis and Clark also showed sincere concern for their men and Sacagawea whenever they got sick or wounded. Clark's compassionate devotion to Sergeant Floyd as he lay dying and Lewis's tender treatment of Sacagawea offer the best two examples. But they also showed their concern in hundreds of other small ways every day. They rested the men when they were tired and treated them for everything from dysentery, boils, constipation, and sore eyes to venereal disease. They did all of this while carrying out their many other responsibilities.

The Glue

All of these characteristics and traits—trust, respect, concern, curiosity, and a willingness to learn, listen, and admit mistakes—helped cultivate the Corps of Discovery. But there was one thing tying everything together, and that was the captains' own unflagging spirit.

When Lewis and Clark reached the Great Falls and saw how difficult the portage would be, they did not complain and they did not waver. When they couldn't find the Shoshone, they never lost confidence. When they peered over the Continental Divide and only saw more mountains, they simply recommitted themselves to their goal. When they grasped the difficulty of the Bitterroots, they marched straight ahead and never considered turning back. And when confronted with the violent rapids of the Columbia, they tackled them with vigor and confidence. By their very outlook and demeanor, Lewis and Clark help infuse the Corps of Discovery with their own unflagging spirit.

Individual Spirit

George Shannon, the youngest member of the expedition, who was lost for almost two weeks in the late summer of 1804, got lost again almost a year later. In this instance, the young soldier was not to blame. The captains had inexplicably sent Shannon down another river on a side excursion and then reversed course without leaving him any information that they had taken this action. To Shannon's great credit, when he didn't meet up with the party at the expected meeting place, he reversed course and went back to the original point of departure. When they weren't there, he correctly surmised that they must have changed plans. Shortly thereafter, he caught back up with the party. I retell this story because it demonstrates how Shannon, in the year that had passed since he first got lost, had gained enough experience and confidence to keep his composure and find his way back.

Another example occurred in the spring of 1806 as the Corps of Discovery was preparing to depart for Fort Clatsop, their camp during the winter of 1805–1806. Food was running low, and the prospect for obtaining more as they headed east for the return trip was remote. Lewis and Clark were in a quandary. They had to get up the river to reconnect with the Indians who were holding their horses. But to reach them, they had to risk starvation. The captains concluded that they had to move forward. What they did next, however, demonstrates the confidence they had developed in every one of the members of the Corps of Discovery. They divided up the last remaining supplies of trading goods and gave each man an equal amount of brass buttons and other trinkets; they then told the men they were responsible for bartering for enough dried fish and roots to sustain themselves over the trip. To a person, everyone was successful.

The final example occurred late in the expedition, shortly after they split up to explore new areas. Before they did so, however, the captains decided that Sergeant Nathaniel Pryor and two other men would travel ahead of the main party to the Mandan villages on an important mission. Shortly after Pryor and his party departed, some Indians stole the group's horses and left them without a mode of transportation. Pryor, now in the middle of the wilderness and far from any help, improvised and fashioned together some buffalo boats (i.e., boats made out of buffalo hides) and advanced up the Yellowstone River. He didn't succeed in his original mission, but he demonstrated enough ingenuity to provide for his small team long enough that they reconnected with the other groups and safely made it back home.

Donning the Cloak of Leadership

These stories demonstrate that one of the primary responsibilities—if not the main responsibility—of any leader is to groom future leaders who are capable of handling difficult and challenging situations when they arise. On this account, Lewis and Clark were very successful. By the time they left the Pacific Coast, they were only halfway through their journey, but they had depleted 95 percent of their supplies. In spite of this fact, Lewis and Clark had so much confidence in their men that once they recrossed the Bitterroots, they divided the party into five different teams and gave each one significant responsibility.

Another testament to Lewis and Clark's ability to groom their men to "don the cloak of leadership" can be seen in what the men of the Corps of Discovery did after the expedition. Nathaniel Pryor became an officer in the Army and served in the Battle of New Orleans. Patrick Gass served in the War of 1812. Reuben Field was offered a lieutenancy by William Clark. And George Shannon, who lost a leg in a later battle, went on to become a successful legislator in Missouri. So instilled was the spirit of the Corps of Discovery that John Colter did not even make it back to St. Louis before venturing back out into the frontier. He requested—and was granted—permission to take leave of the party in August 1806. He would later go on to become the first American to discover Yellowstone National Park. And George Droulliard, John Potts, and Peter Weiser would also return to the frontier to help Manuel Lisa, a noted fur trader and frontier explorer, establish American trading posts. (All three, however, paid the ultimate price and later died in violent conflicts with the Blackfeet Indians.)

Leading Into the Unknown

Explorers are a frequent source of inspiration for business leaders, and outdoor wilderness experiences have proved to be a popular method for companies attempting to build or improve cooperation and teamwork. The goal-oriented nature of exploration, together with the challenging terrain and the constantly changing conditions, closely parallels what businesses—and particularly business leaders—face on a daily basis. Lewis and Clark's experiences therefore offer a number of valuable lessons that executives can apply to help cultivate a Corps of Discovery within their own organization.

Lead by example. There is no indication that Lewis or Clark ever spoke about or even consciously thought about developing "team spirit." It was just something they did—and they started by leading with their own example. They gave up their comfortable lives, diligently prepared themselves, shared leadership, selected only the best personnel, and did the scores of other, smaller things that demonstrated that they were absolutely committed to the mission and that the success of the mission was paramount.

The wave of corporate scandals that have rocked America in recent years suggests that some business leaders have fallen far from the path of leading by example. The goal of any organization—

including business—is not to serve oneself; it is to serve the share-holders and, more important, society at large. In his book *Good to Great*, Jim Collins writes about "Level 5 Leadership," which he defines as an executive who builds greatness through personal humility and professional will. A close review of the characteristics that define this type of leadership will reveal that Lewis and Clark possessed almost every characteristic, including their reliance on "inspired standards."

Start early and demonstrate trust. Lewis and Clark, upon dis-embarking from Camp Dubois, immediately put their main party in the same boat. The implied message was that they were all in it together and needed to work together as a team to succeed. More important, Lewis and Clark demonstrated a great degree of trust early on by allowing the men to select the replacement for Sergeant Floyd. An excellent example of a company that demonstrates trust in its employees is Northwestern Mutual. Employees are not given extensive and detailed instructions to aid them in making every decision; rather, they are given the simple advice to "do whatever is in the customer's best interest" and then are given the authority to act within those broad parameters.

Celebrate success. As recounted in Chapter Five, Lewis and Clark often took the time to recognize and reward individual effort as well as celebrate team success. They did the former by naming rivers and streams in honor of their members, and the latter by giving the team an occasional day of rest or issuing some extra whiskey and letting everyone sing and dance for an evening. The captains' actions were the equivalent of a leader today finding a way to publicly honor the effort of employees or giving them time off in recognition of a job well done. The advice might seem obvious, but in an environment where larger and more significant milestones or goals lie beyond the horizon, it is easy to give in to the temptation not to celebrate until the final or ultimate goal is achieved. The problem with this approach is that new goals often have a way of materializing. Furthermore, leaders who adopt this approach often lose excellent opportunities to bolster the morale of their employees—which is so vital in helping companies achieve the next goal or milestone.

Change with the conditions. New environments and new experiences require different managerial styles. After Lewis and Clark left Fort Mandan and started the second leg of their journey, they put away the whip for good and instead relied on positive reinforcement as their preferred managerial tool. Businesses will also have different needs and concerns depending on the unique demands and particular needs of a given situation. The responsibility of a leader is to be sensitive to these changing conditions and respond accordingly. For instance, when a business is facing stiff competition or a bleak economic scenario, a leader may need to take quick, decisive, unilateral action, whereas decisions during more prosperous times, or decisions on how to best enter a new market or introduce a new product, may benefit from a more collaborative approach. The bottom line is that Lewis and Clark understood that there was no one leadership style that worked in all situations.

Be willing to listen. At the Marias, the captains overruled their men. This didn't mean that they didn't listen to them. By giving the men an opportunity to share their opinions, they let the members of the Corps of Discovery at least feel that they had been heard. The lesson is that even though Lewis and Clark made a unilateral decision, they minimized internal dissent by listening to the counterarguments and explaining to their team why they disagreed with their analysis. Contrast this with an executive who simply makes a decision and provides no explanation for the decision. Not only are employees likely to be less motivated to execute the decision, they may actively work to undermine it. Both have negative implications for the morale of the team and the success of the mission.

Don't dwell on mistakes. The unknown, by its very nature, is a messy place. Not every contingency can be foreseen and things change. By refusing to view mistakes as anything other than learning opportunities, Lewis and Clark ensured that the Corps of Discovery felt comfortable innovating and trying new things. Inflexibility—especially in the wilderness—was a recipe for disaster.

In Chapter Nine, I wrote about the infamous "New Coke" fiasco. What happened after the company pulled the plug on the product is also telling—perhaps even more revealing than its decision to reverse course. In spite of many calls for then-CEO Roberto Goizueta and his team to be fired, the chairman of the compensation committee for Coca-Cola's board of directors *rewarded* Goizueta with $1.7 million in salary and almost $5 million in stock options. When asked why he did it, the chairman replied, "They had the courage to put their jobs on the line, and that's rarely done today at major American companies." Put another way, a firing would have put everyone at Coca-Cola on notice that risk taking was something to be punished. The committee had the good sense to recognize and understand that the longer-term consequences of such an action would be disastrous to the company's long-term performance.

Demonstrate genuine concern. The wilderness, like the unknown, can be a forbidding place. People can and will get roughed up. As leaders, Lewis and Clark acknowledged these realities and, to the best of their ability, treated their team with concern and compassion. In doing so, they not only met a human need, but also allowed the members of the Corps of Discovery to concentrate on their respective jobs. In today's workplace, companies are confronted with their employees' real concerns about health care, child-rearing responsibilities, and maybe even having to care for an elderly parent. Some of the issues may be beyond the capacity of business executives to do anything about, but they can still acknowledge that they are at least aware of the issues. This simple act of acknowledging the concerns of employees can go a long way toward developing a sense of team. Of course, if it is within the power of the company to actually do something constructive to help the employee (e.g., by offering paid benefits, flex time, parental or family medical leave, etc.), the effect will likely be even greater—and it may even have a positive impact on the bottom line by freeing employees to concentrate on their jobs.

One such example of a leader demonstrating concern—or showing some empathy—for his employees is Herb Baum. When he was CEO of Quaker State (before its acquisition by Shell Oil), he received permission from the board to disperse his own bonus of $155,000 among the 155 lowest-paid employees, whom he knew were having a hard time paying their own bills. The act went a long way toward fostering a sense of team spirit at the company.

Do the little things. Lewis and Clark never hesitated to share in the daily burdens of the journey. Their actions did more than just lighten the load of the others. They signified that the mission was paramount and showed that the captains understood what everyone else was doing. In the business world, Lewis and Clark's actions would be the equivalent of a CEO flying coach or giving up a coveted corner office or privileged parking space. An example of an executive doing the small things is Herb Kelleher, CEO of Southwest Airlines. The Wednesday before every Thanksgiving (the busiest traveling day of the year), he spends the entire day loading and unloading baggage. It might not appear to be the most productive use of a CEO's time, but when one considers the effect on morale and its contribution to the sense of teamwork at Southwest, it is quite possibly the most productive time Kelleher spends each year.

Groom future leaders. Lewis and Clark started from the premise that individuals could handle responsibility, instead of first making them earn it. Almost without exception, the members of the Corps of Discovery demonstrated that they were capable of handling ever-increasing amounts of responsibility. This trust contributed to the success of the mission because it allowed the captains to focus their time and talent elsewhere and gave team members the skills, experience, and confidence they would need to become leaders themselves. In this way, Lewis and Clark were able to continue their legacy because so many members of the Corps of Discovery went back out into the wilderness to help settle the American West.

Jack Welch, the legendary former CEO of General Electric Company, has often said that GE's core competency is its people-building approach to teams and leader development. During his tenure, Welch did not just pay lip service to these ideals; he actively worked to develop leaders by building up GE's Management Development Institute (now known as the John F. Welch

Leadership Center). The leaders who studied at the institute—many of whom Welch personally trained—not only have gone on to lead other multinational companies, but were the primary reason Welch was able to add $450 billion to GE's market capitalization during his twenty years with the company. The point is that people truly are a company's most valuable resource.

Proceed On!

In giving York and Sacagawea the right to vote on where to establish their winter camp in 1805, Lewis and Clark preceded their country by 65 and 115 years, respectively, in recognizing that every person, regardless of race or sex, brings real value to a team. That it took the crucible of exploration—particularly the exploration of the unknown—to come to this realization serves as a reminder that whatever the future might hold, it can only be conquered by individuals who have been given the opportunity to discover their full value. Only then will individuals quickly realize that even greater things can be accomplished by working in partnership with others as a team. And that, in the end, is what it really means to cultivate a Corps of Discovery—to discover greatness in a team.

EPILOGUE

The mind of man is capable of anything—
because everything is in it, all the past as
well as all the future.

                    —Joseph Conrad

David Lavender begins his book *The Way to the Western Sea: Lewis and Clark Across the Continent* with the word *luck*. Stephen Ambrose entitled his book about the expedition *Undaunted Courage*. James Ronda in *Lewis and Clark Among the Indians* makes a compelling case that the natives were essential to Lewis and Clark's success. Each writer is correct. Luck, courage, and the native Indians all played vital roles in the success of the Corps of Discovery. So did a number of other factors—including everything from the unique abilities of the individual members of the Corps of Discovery to Thomas Jefferson's vision for the expedition. In the end, however, there was one constant through-out the arduous twenty-eight-month, 8,000-mile expedition and that was the leadership of Meriwether Lewis and William Clark.

There is an age-old question of whether leaders are born or made. It is a false debate. The truth contains elements of both. There can be no denying that by virtue of their upbringing and background, Lewis and Clark were born into leadership. Their experiences and education qualified them to be officers in the Army, and their connections provided them access to mentors who refined their skills and gave them opportunities not available to others.

However, there were three other official and unofficial attempts by the United States to reach the Pacific before Lewis and Clark—and all failed. Moreover, many of the subsequent expeditions that followed Lewis and Clark also ended in failure. The captains were uniquely successful. They possessed something more—something intangible. Many management books today will talk about *authoritative* leadership, *participative* leadership, *consensual* and *autocratic* leadership, as well as dozens of other types of leadership—and they will often speak as though people can only possess one style. Lewis and Clark intuitively knew that there was no one type of leadership. As required, they were authoritative and participative, consensual and autocratic. Lewis and Clark had an amazing set of talents, and much like an expert golfer knows to pull out just the right club according to the distinct demands of a given situation, they deftly knew just when and how to employ each of those talents.

They were visionary and practical. They balanced daily needs with long-term concerns, compassion with discipline, risk analysis with gut instinct, forced marches with rest and relaxation. They improvised as necessary, made mistakes without imploding, and shared leadership without ever giving it away. Through it all, they remained optimistic in the face of incredible odds.

In their hearts, however, they were explorers, and the crucible of exploration required that they keep learning, adapting, and improving. It is this lesson that serves to remind us that leaders are not so much made as they are forged in the crucible of their experiences.

In the end, however, regardless of whether leaders are born, forged, or developed through some combination of factors, the thing that matters most is results. Leaders are judged on results. And on that account, Lewis and Clark were wildly successful. Even though they failed in their primary goal to find an all-water route to the Pacific, they opened the American West, secured the land for the United States, and made our future possible. Along the way they made many other discoveries—the greatest of which was the discovery of their team. Their confidence soared as they moved west, and it gave them the strength to proceed on just a little more each day until they got the job done. And they did it in a way that made the journey almost seem easy.

The reason they were successful is because in the face of great uncertainty, Lewis and Clark had clear principles. These principles helped them blaze a bold course into an unknown future and gave them the confidence they needed to succeed. To recapitulate, these ten principles are:

→ Passionate Purpose: The Principle of a Higher Calling

→ Productive Partnering: The Principle of Shared Leadership

→ Future Think: The Principle of Strategic Preparation

→ Honoring Differences: The Principle of Diversity

↪ Equitable Justice: The Principle of Compassionate Discipline

↪ Absolute Responsibility: The Principle of Leading from the Front

↪ Meaningful Mentoring: The Principle of Learning from Others

↪ Realistic Optimism: The Principle of Positive Thinking

↪ Rational Risk: The Principle of Aggressive Analysis

↪ Cultivating a Corps of Discovery: The Principle of Developing Team Spirit

On April 7, 1805, just as Meriwether Lewis was poised to leave from Fort Mandan and depart for that portion of the journey where the map was literally a blank, he wrote that his mind was "suffered to wander into futurity" and that the journey he was about to undertake was "a most pleasing one . . . I could but esteem this moment of departure as among the most happy of my life." Although he was on the brink of the unknown, he wasn't concerned, nervous, or scared—Meriwether Lewis was happy!

By applying the ten principles of Lewis and Clark, you too can "proceed on" and chart a course that will happily guide you into the unknown, confident that the unknown can be conquered and that the future is not so much meant to be discovered as it is meant to be created.

APPENDIX A

Members of the Corps of Discovery

THE PERMANENT PARTY
Members of the permanent party were those who departed from
Fort Mandan in the spring of 1805 and reached the Pacific. There
were thirty-three permanent party members:

CAPTAINS
Meriwether Lewis

William Clark

SERGEANTS
Patrick Gass

John Ordway

Nathaniel Pryor

PRIVATES

William Bratton

John Collins

John Colter

Pierre Cruzatte

Joseph Field

Reuben Field

Robert Frazier

George Gibson

Silas Goodrich

Hugh Hall

Thomas Howard

Francois Labiche

John Baptiste LePage

Hugh McNeal

John Potts

George Shannon

John Shields

John Thompson

Peter Weiser

William Werner

Joseph Whitehouse

Alexander Willard

Richard Windsor

CIVILIANS

Jean Baptiste Charbonneau
  (Pomp)

Toussaint Charbonneau

George Droulliard

Sacagawea

York

INDIVIDUALS WHO MADE A PORTION OF THE TRIP

John Boley

John Dame

Charles Floyd (died)

John Newman (disbanded)

Moses Reed (disbanded)

John Robertson

Ebenezer Tuttle

Richard Warfington

Isaac White

FRENCH ENGAGES

These French boatmen were hired to help the expedition navigate the first leg of the journey up the Missouri:

Jean Baptiste DeChamps

Jean Baptiste La Jeunnesse

Joseph Barter

Alexander Carson

Charles Caugee

Joseph Collin

Charles Hebert

Etienne Malbouf

Peter Pinaut

Paul Primeau

Francois Rivet

Peter Roi

NOTES

1. Robert B. Betts, "'we commenced wrighting & c': A Salute to the Ingenious Spelling and Grammar of William Clark," *We Proceeded On*, vol. 6, no. 4 (November 1980), p. 10.

2. Stephen E. Ambrose, *Undaunted Courage: Meriwether Lewis, Thomas Jefferson, and the Opening of the American West* (New York: Simon & Schuster, 1996), p. 200.

3. Dayton Duncan and Ken Burns, *Lewis and Clark: An Illustrated History* (New York: Alfred Knopf, 1997), p. ix.

4. Robert R. Hunt, "Luck or Providence: Narrow Escapes on the Lewis and Clark Expedition," *We Proceeded On*, vol. 25, no. 3 (August 1999), p. 7.

5. Dayton Duncan, "What the Lewis and Clark Expedition Means to America," *We Proceeded On*, vol. 23, no. 3 (August 1997), p. 6.

CHAPTER 1

1. David Lavender, *The Way to the Western Sea: Lewis and Clark Across the Continent* (Lincoln, NE: University of Nebraska Press, 2001), p. 18.

2. Stephen E. Ambrose, *Undaunted Courage: Meriwether Lewis, Thomas Jefferson, and the Opening of the American West* (New York: Simon & Schuster, 1996), pp. 20–21.

3. Jerome Steffen, *William Clark: Jeffersonian Man on the Frontier* (Norman, OK: University of Oklahoma, 1997), p. 15.

4. Ambrose, *Undaunted Courage*, pp. 20–21.

5. William George, *Leading with Your Values* (Minneapolis, MN: Center for Ethical Business Cultures, 1993).

6. Seth Shulman, "The Vision Thing," *Technology Review* (May 2003), p. 75.

7. Frederick F. Reichheld, "Lead for Loyalty," *Harvard Business Review* (July-August 2001), p. 80.

8. Bette Price, "Values Shift Requires Leadership," *Business Facilities* (November 2001); available at http://www.facilitycity. com/busfac/bf_01_11_workforce2.asp.

CHAPTER 2

1. Stephen E. Ambrose, *Undaunted Courage: Meriwether Lewis, Thomas Jefferson, and the Opening of the American West* (New York: Simon & Schuster, 1996), p. 249. In his book, Ambrose attributes this theory on Clark's displeasure with the iron boat project to Arlen Large.

CHAPTER 3

1. James P. Ronda, *Lewis and Clark Among the Indians* (Lincoln, NE: University of Nebraska Press, 1984), p. 14.

2. Stephen E. Ambrose, *Undaunted Courage: Meriwether Lewis, Thomas Jefferson, and the Opening of the American West* (New York: Simon & Schuster, 1996), p. 106.

3. Peter Schwartz, *The Art of the Long View: Paths to Strategic Insights for Yourself and Your Company* (New York: Doubleday, 1996).

CHAPTER 4

1. Carol Lynn MacGregor, "The Role of the Gass Journal," *We Proceeded On* (November 1990), pp. 13–17.

2. Robert E. Lange, "George Droulliard (Drewyer): One of the Two or Three Most Valuable Men on the Expedition," *We Proceeded On* (May 1979), p. 14.

3. Robert B. Betts, *In Search of York: The Slave Who Went to the Pacific with Lewis and Clark* (Boulder, CO: University Press of Colorado, 1985); and James J. Holmberg, "York's Post-Expedition Life and Estrangement from William Clark" (epilogue to Robert Betts, *In Search of York*, revised edition 2002), pp. 151–170.

CHAPTER 5

1. James P. Ronda, "A Most Perfect Harmony—Life at Fort Mandan," *We Proceeded On* (November 1988), pp. 4–9.

2. Ronald A. Heifetz and Marty Linsky, "A Survival Guide for Leaders," *Harvard Business Review* (June 2002), p. 70.

CHAPTER 6

1. Stephen E. Ambrose, *Undaunted Courage: Meriwether Lewis, Thomas Jefferson, and the Opening of the American West* (New York: Simon & Schuster, 1996), p. 230.

CHAPTER 7

1. Bernard DeVoto, *The Journals of Lewis and Clark* (New York: Houghton Mifflin Company, 1953), p. liv.

2. Jerome O. Steffen, *William Clark: Jeffersonian Man on the Frontier* (Norman, OK: University of Oklahoma, 1997), pp. 22–23.

3. Coy Barefoot, *Thomas Jefferson on Leadership: Executive Lessons from His Life and Letters* (New York: Plume, 2002), p. 167.

4. Stephen E. Ambrose, *Undaunted Courage: Meriwether Lewis, Thomas Jefferson, and the Opening of the American West* (New York: Simon & Schuster, 1996), p. 57.

5. Steffen, *William Clark: Jeffersonian Man on the Frontier,* pp. 22–23.

6. Ambrose, *Undaunted Courage*, p. 57.

7. Jennifer Reingold, "Want to Grow as a Leader? Get a Mentor!" *Fast Company* (January 2001), p. 58.

8. "The Long—but Not Lonely—Road to Success," *Indianapolis Business Journal* (February 15, 1999), p. 8.

9. Barry Sweeney, "What Results Does Mentoring Deliver?" available at http://198.66.196.166/ResultsOfM.html.

CHAPTER 8

1. John Logan Allen, "Summer of Decision: Lewis and Clark in Montana, 1805," *We Proceeded On*, vol. 8, no. 4 (Fall 1976), p. 10.

2. Martin Seligman, *Learned Optimism: How to Change Your Mind and Your Life* (New York: Free Press, 1998).

CHAPTER 9

1. Kathleen M. Sutcliffe and Klaus Weber, "The High Cost of Accurate Knowledge," *Harvard Business Review* (May 2003), pp. 75–82.

2. Gary Hamel and Eric Schonfeld, "Why It's Time to Take a Risk," *Business 2.0* (April 2003), p. 68.

CHAPTER 10

1. Stephen E. Ambrose, *Undaunted Courage: Meriwether Lewis, Thomas Jefferson, and the Opening of the American West* (New York: Simon & Schuster, 1996), p. 298.

2. Ambrose, *Undaunted Courage*, p. 165.

3. Herb Baum, "Moving Mountains," *Harvard Business Review* (January 2003), p. 45.

RESOURCES

Books

Allen, John Logan. *Passage Through the Garden: Lewis and Clark and the Image of the American Northwest.* Urbana, IL: University of Illinois Press, 1975.

Ambrose, Stephen E. *Undaunted Courage: Meriwether Lewis, Thomas Jefferson, and the Opening of the American West.* New York: Simon & Schuster, 1996.

Betts, Robert B. *In Search of York: The Slave Who Went to the Pacific with Lewis and Clark.* Boulder, CO: University Press of Colorado, 1985.

Chuinard, Eldon. *Only One Man Died: The Medical Aspects of the Lewis and Clark Expedition.* Glendale, CA: Arthur Clark Company, 1980.

Clarke, Charles G. *The Men of the Lewis and Clark Expedition.* Lincoln, NE: University of Nebraska Press, 1970.

Cutright, Paul Russel. *Lewis and Clark: Pioneering Naturalists.* Urbana, IL: University of Illinois Press, 1986.

DeVoto, Bernard., ed. *The Journals of Lewis and Clark*. New York: Houghton Mifflin Company, 1953.

Dillon, Richard. *Meriwether Lewis: A Biography*. New York: Coward-McCann, 1965.

Duncan, Dayton, and Ken Burns. *Lewis and Clark: An Illustrated History*. New York: Alfred Knopf, 1997.

Gass, Patrick. *A Journal of the Voyages and Travels of a Corps of Discovery Under the Command of Capt. Lewis and Capt. Clark*. Minneapolis: Ross and Haines, 1958.

Howard, Harold P. *Sacajawea*. Norman, OK: University of Oklahoma Press, 1971.

Jackson, Donald., ed. *Letters of the Lewis and Clark Expedition*. Urbana, IL: University of Illinois Press, 1978.

Lavender, David. *The Way to the Western Sea: Lewis and Clark Across the Continent*. Lincoln, NE: University of Nebraska Press, 2001.

Moulton, Gary. *The Journals of the Lewis & Clark Expedition*, vol. 1–13. Lincoln, NE: University of Nebraska Press, 1986–1993.

Ronda, James P. *Lewis and Clark Among the Indians*. Lincoln, NE: University of Nebraska Press, 1984.

Schmidt, Thomas, and Jeremy Schmidt. *The Saga of Lewis and Clark: Into the Uncharted West*. New York: DK Publishing, 1999.

Steffen, Jerome O. *William Clark: Jeffersonian Man on the Frontier*. Norman, OK: University of Oklahoma, 1977.

Thomasma, Kenneth. *The Truth About Sacajawea.* Jackson, WY: Grandview Publishing Company, 1997.

Periodicals and Magazines

We Proceeded On, The Quarterly Journal of the Lewis and Clark Trail Heritage Foundation, PO Box 3434, Great Falls, MT 59403, Phone: 888-701-3434.

Videos and Web Sites

Discovering Lewis and Clark (http://www.lewis-clark.org/). Interactive multimedia program based on a multi-part synopsis of the expedition's story by historian Harry W. Fritz.

Lewis & Clark: The Journey of the Corps of Discovery, A Film by Ken Burns. PBS Home Video. Available in video/DVD formats at shopPBS.org or at PBS Online (http://www.pbs.org/lewisand-clark/).

Lewis and Clark Trail Heritage Foundation, Inc. (http://www.lewisandclark.org/). Publishes *We Proceeded On* and supplemental books about the Corps of Discovery.

National Geographic's Lewis and Clark Interactive Journal Log (http://www.nationalgeographic.com/lewisandclark/).

The Lewis and Clark Journey of Discovery (http://www.nps.gov/jeff/LewisClark2/HomePage/HomePage.htm). An online presentation of the Jefferson National Expansion Memorial of the National Park Service.

INDEX

ABOUT THE AUTHOR

Jack Uldrich is a writer, speaker, and business consultant. He is the president of The NanoVeritas Group, an international consultancy dedicated to assisting businesses and governments to understand, prepare for, and profit from nanotechnology. He is also the author of *The Next Big Thing Is Really Small: How Nanotechnology Will Change the Future of Your Business*. He previously served as the deputy director of the Minnesota Office of Strategic and Long Range Planning in the administration of Governor Jesse Ventura. He is a former naval intelligence officer and worked as a civilian policy adviser in the Pentagon. From 2001 to 2003, he served as the chairman of the Independence Party of Minnesota. He lives in Minneapolis with his wife and their two children, and can be reached at jack@nanoveritas.com.

DATE DUE		
JUN 3 0 2004		
MAY 26 2005 DEC 1 3 2004		